God in La La Land
A Christian Perspective

Randy Lovejoy

Andrew Wood, editor

Endorsements

God in La La Land by Randy Lovejoy is a love song to the mystique of Los Angeles. Delving deep into the city's history, Lovejoy brings forth anecdotal gems, like the story of Biddy Mason, a freed slave who donated land to build a church. Los Angeles is where anything can happen. This history of Christianity in Los Angeles looks specifically at the ways dreams, hopes, and spirituality are part of the DNA of the city. Throughout all the dreams searched for, fulfilled, or unfulfilled, we see the transcendence of the Holy Spirit at work in this particular place. *God in La La Land* is a must-read for planters and pastors in the Los Angeles area who want to understand the rich history of Christianity in their context.

Dr. Robert E. Logan
author of *The Discipleship Difference*.

As a recording artist & performer, LA has always seemed full of contradictions to me, it is a place of mystical creativity, a home for the weird and wonderful, yet it also can feel like a rat-race for those in the entertainment industry. The external and sometimes superficial face of LA can blind one to the wealth of spiritual wisdom, tradition, ritual and stories that helped create the city we know today. Randy's exploration into the longing for transcendence which has punctuated culture in Los Angeles for decades helps one to gain a larger context for the city and therefore appreciate all it has to offer.

Kimbra
Singer/Songwriter
www.kimbramusic.com

Los Angeles is a city with a history – and a destiny. But how do we grasp the true meaning of the City of Angels? Randy Lovejoy seeks a transcending narrative by going through LA's Christian history to help us develop a greater understanding of the city's spiritual birth so that meaningful dialogue can begin for its future. Beginning with the spiritual worldview of the Native Americans and its collision with the Spanish spiritual worldview during the conquest and followed by the manifest destiny spirituality that drove the early development of the United States, Rev. Lovejoy presents us with a mosaic of forces, examples, and Biblical paradigms that will help the reader grasp the complexities in ministering in a large urban mission field with a vision and hope for the future.

Dr. Duane "Chip" Anderson
CEO
Christ For the City International

The theme of the city in Scripture is a study in itself. This fascinating book provides glimpses of the Christian faith in the life of one major American city over centuries from the First Nations to the present day. It is a splendid beginning to what promises to be an important series.

Andrew F Walls

University of Edinburgh and Liverpool Hope University

Good urban missiology requires, first, a deep understanding and appreciation for one's own context (both the historical and emerging influences within our cities). Second, it requires an attentiveness to the complexity of the network of subcultures at work around us - which each come with their own bridges and barriers to understanding the gospel message. Finally, it requires a love and respect for the questions of spiritual seekers in our midst. In his new work, *God in La La Land,* Randy Lovejoy not only brings together each of these elements, but does so in a way which will hopefully spark the creative imaginations of those both within and outside of the church. For any ministry looking to more effectively reach Los Angeles, I'd recommend this work as an important resource in creating your mission's strategy.

Seth Bouchelle
NYC Team Leader for Global City Mission Initiative
Author of *Mosaic.*

Randy Lovejoy has provided a robust and gripping narrative for those interested in the history of the Church in Los Angeles. His research gives a solid ground for learning relevant information about how God has moved amongst God's people in Southern California and Randy writes in such a way that readers are held through the compelling story telling. If you are interested in this topic, Lovejoy's work is an essential

Nick Warnes
Executive Director of Cyclical LA
Pastor of Northland Village Church in Los Angeles.

Lovejoy

In *God in La La Land: A Christian Perspective,* Randy Lovejoy uses the lens of sociological history to explore the role of Christianity in today's urban center. The theological reflections surrounding marginalization, inclusion, vision, incarnational presence, and more are must reads for all those leading faith communities in the 21st century, but especially those in urban ministry. Lovejoy's keen eye for detail and nuance helps him underscore parallels between LA's history and Biblical scenarios. In so doing, he makes both the Bible and present-day ministry come alive with new understanding. This book should be used as a template for authors and practical theologians in every community, but short of that, reading Randy's book will provide a blueprint for redefining the church for today's world in communities across the nation.

The Reverend Deborah Fae Swift

M.S., M.Div.

Pastor of South Presbyterian Church in Rochester, NY

creator of the Acts of Faith Model of Ministry.

Throughout these pages I discovered an increasing sense of hope and reverence for the hidden spiritual depths of Los Angeles that are so easy to miss amidst the chaos and superficialities for which it is often maligned. The warmth of the personal narrative woven seamlessly with accessible, impeccable research helped me connect on multiple levels to a web of people on diverse faith explorations—and that is truly invaluable in providing the solidarity and inspiration necessary to keep my own vibrant and sturdy in a city that fosters isolation and daily demands I prove my worth through fame. Here is an opportunity to both fall in love with wild Los Angeles and her never static opportunities on the spiritual margins and also to feel released to honor our inner wildness that wants to jump into the messiness and glory together with God and neighbor of learning to love and be loved in the city of Angeles. If you're looking for a tour bus through the landmarks & off the beaten path spirituality in Los Angeles, this will be the curious, exciting book to transport you and then drop you off at your front door with so many ideas for engaging your spirituality right in your own city context.

Cat Moore
Artist and Writer
Community Developer.

Randy Lovejoy has captured our imagination. When we see what God has done in the past through Randy's animated posts and descriptive blog entries that carry us leaping through time, we just might come to believe that God is indeed able to do similar things now and in the future, maybe even through ourselves. This is a must-read for every Christian looking for hope. Hope that God can bring renewal to our families, our neighborhoods, our communities and our nation. Hope that God can bring renewal through ordinary people living ordinary lives who are willing to risk letting God lead them in new ways, into the communities and lives of the many peoples seeking hope. "Take it and read," as Augustine heard and so did and so was changed.

James Milley

Chief Catalyst, Bridges

Randy Lovejoy has taken a complex sociological phenomenon, called the city and through his experience in Los Angeles, given us insight into both his and our spiritual journeys. Margins provides a wonderful Biblical world view analysis and exhortation that guarantees to challenge our vision and hope for the mission field, most culturally diverse and available to us today. Read only if you want to be challenged to see missions and ministry in a new meaningful way that will call you to action.

Sam Voorhies

President/CEO of Voorhies Consulting

Lovejoy

God in La La Land

A Christian Perspective

Urban Loft Publishers
P.O. Box 6
Skyforest, CA 92385
www.urbanloftpublishers.com

Senior Editors: Stephen Burris & Kendi Howells Douglas
Copy Editor: Christian Arnold
Track Editor: Andrew Wood
Graphics: Morgan Simms
Photo Credits: Randy Lovejoy, Shuttershock, Pexels, & Cat Moore

ISBN-13: 978-0-9989177-9-5

Made in the U.S

Series Preface

Urban Mission in the 21st Century is a series of monographs that addresses key issues facing those involved in urban ministry whether it be in the slums, squatter communities, *favelas*, or in immigrant neighborhoods. It is our goal to bring fresh ideas, a theological basis, and best practices in urban mission as we reflect on our changing urban world. The contributors to this series bring a wide-range of ideas, experiences, education, international perspectives, and insight into the study of the growing field of urban ministry. These contributions fall into four very general areas: 1--the biblical and theological basis for urban ministry; 2--best practices currently in use and anticipated in the future by urban scholar/activists who are living working and studying in the context of cities; 3--personal experiences and observations based on urban ministry as it is currently being practiced; and 4--a forward view toward where we are headed in the decades ahead in the expanding and developing field of urban mission. This series is intended for educators, graduate students, theologians, pastors, and serious students of urban ministry.

More than anything, these contributions are creative attempts to help Christians strategically and creatively think about how we can better reach our world that is now more urban than rural. We do not see theology and practice as separate and distinct. Rather, we see sound practice growing out of a healthy vibrant theology that seeks to understand God's world as it truly is as we move further into the twenty-first century. Contributors interact with the best scholarly literature available at the time of writing while making application to specific contexts in which they live and work.

Each book in the series is intended to be a thought-provoking work that represents the author's experience and perspective on urban ministry in a particular context. The editors have chosen those who bring this rich diversity of perspectives to this series. It is our hope and prayer that each book in this series will challenge, enrich, provoke, and cause the reader to dig deeper into subjects that bring the reader to a deeper understanding of our urban world and the ministry the church is called to perform in that new world.

Dr. Kendi Howells Douglas and Stephen Burris,
Urban Mission in the 21st Century Series Co-Editors

Acknowledgments

"We are like dwarfs on the shoulders of giants..."

John of Salisbury

The Metalogicon (1159) bk. 3, ch. 4

I have, at times, felt guilty writing this book. At first I thought that this book was supposed be an expression of my own creativity. But the deeper I got into this project the more I was forced to face the fact that this book was being written on the shoulders of many others who have gone before me.

Eventually the guilt has given way to grace. I have become deeply grateful for the extensive community, both living and dead, who have contributed to this work. In gratitude, I would like to acknowledge some of the people who deserve special thanks. Three people with far greater knowledge and experience of Los Angeles kindly gave time for interviews early on, Dr. Mel Robeck, Rev. Alexia Salvatierra, and Dr. Jude Tiersma opened my eyes to many things in this city, far too many for me to include in this short book, but more than enough to motivate me to complete the manuscript. Thanks also to John Brady and Laura Mullen, two friends who brainstormed with me one morning as we walked around the Silver Lake reservoir until we came up with the title of the book. And thank you to three people who helped me with detail work on the book. The Rev. Ken Baker read an early chapter and offered suggestions. Dianne Russell worked in detail with every chapter and endnote of the book as well as the appendices. Cheryl Lovejoy, my wonderful wife, read each chapter and offered critical advice. Finally, I would like to thank Dr. Andrew Walls, who first recommended me to Urban Loft, Dr. Stephen Burris, who opened up this opportunity and Dr. Kendi Howells Douglas, who walked me through the whole process. Thanks to everyone! You have proven that life is infinitely more complex and more blessed than I had ever assumed.

Randy Lovejoy

Los Angeles, CA

Table of Contents

General Introduction to the Series

The Bible begins with a picture of a garden; it ends with a picture of a city. The latter picture is remarkably detailed; we are told of the variety of splendid materials used in the construction of its walls and streets, of the remarkable river which flows through its center, and--lest we assume that with so much gold and jeweled magnificence it might be hot and glaring--we are told of the shady trees with their varied fruit and their healing leaves. It is a cosmopolitan city, and a safe one. It stands foursquare, with equal numbers of gates on each side, all open day and night. Constant traffic comes through those gates: the richest treasures of all the nations, whether to the north, south, east or west, while evil things do not enter at all.

Not surprisingly, the holy city as described in the last two chapters of the book of Revelation, has been taken as a depiction of heaven. But John clearly indicates that it is a depiction of the Church; "Come" says his guiding angel, "and I will show you the Bride, the wife of the Lamb" (Revelation 21:9). The holy city is the Church as it is in principle, and as it will be in the end time.

So, in the New Testament, we find a city, the ideal city, is the model of the Church. That city is large and populous, with shared amenities (like the flowing river and the healing trees) for its citizens and including among those citizens people from all over the world. Furthermore, it is an actual, historically existing city that has been transformed; it is the New Jerusalem. Old Jerusalem had a long history; it had been a Jebusite city before David captured it and made it an Israelite city. On various occasions it had been besieged, captured, plundered, devastated. But in the New Jerusalem there are no ruins or damaged places to be seen. Old Jerusalem had a fragile water supply; the New Jerusalem has that river flowing from the throne of God.

11

From Solomon's time to AD 70, the great architectural glory of old Jerusalem had been the temple of God; but that temple was ethnically restricted and in the New Jerusalem, with its gates open to all the world, no temple building is needed --God is with his people and the whole city becomes his temple. Old Jerusalem has been completely rebuilt in heaven.

This is not the only place in the New Testament where the city is used as a model of the redemptive purposes of God. In the Epistle to the Hebrews, as the author sets out his theme of faith demonstrated in the scriptures of the Old Testament, he describes the faithful of Old Testament times as migrants seeking a city, assuring us that God had in fact already prepared a city for them, one with permanent foundations. He also makes it clear that the city they sought is to be shared with those who come after them to faith in Jesus Christ.

That the city prepared for the migrants and the city renewed and transformed are such powerful New Testament images makes this series of volumes on the Christian significance of cities across the continents a project both important and timely. Cities represent human activities in their most intensive form whether in industry and production, in commerce, trade and finance, in building and construction, in education and learning, in the arts and music, and not least in religion. Cities contain people from many places beyond their boundaries, both from the surrounding area and from far away, all of whom will have had their own reasons for seeking what the author of Hebrews calls "a better country." And as the Law of Moses reminds us, cities may also be respected places of sanctuary.

Accordingly, cities commonly have many communities within one civic community. They have layers of administration and government. Frequently they are home to both opulence and squalor, historic monuments and recent innovations, growth and decay, affluence and deprivation. In Christian understanding, Christ is to be made known in all these settings, and we have seen that the New Testament gives profound significance to the concept of the city and is suggestive of its redemption and transformation. This series can help us to ponder these things further as we gain some acquaintance with some of the greatest cities of the Americas, Europe, Asia and Africa, in every case with a guide who knows it intimately and loves it well, and can introduce us to both its present and its past, and can explain both the city's Christian history and how Christ lives there today. In our journeys around these cities we are likely to learn much about human life and its patterns of community. We shall also have reason to reflect on God's choice of a historic city as the model of the Church, and of the ways in which the New Jerusalem may represent the redemption of the city. "The leaves of the tree are for the healing of the nations."

Andrew F. Walls

Honorary Professor, University of Edinburgh

Visiting Professor, Akrofi-Christaller Institute of Theology, Mission and Culture, Ghana

Founding editor of the *Journal of Religion in Africa*

Lovejoy

Introduction to the Series

"Jesus spoke all these things to the crowd in parables; he
did not say anything to them without using a parable."
Matthew 13:34

Jesus is known for telling stories. His stories were set in the events of ordinary life. But their unexpected turns have caught people's attention for millennia. Our cities tell similar stories, if we have ears to hear. Each volume in this series shares stories from a particular city which, like Jesus' parables, are a source of wisdom for our everyday lives.

But gaining such insight is challenging. Human life can lose a sense of meaning in the city. A vast sea of humanity comes and goes on a daily basis, year after year, generation after generation, wave after wave after wave. This tidal ebb and flow erodes individual purpose and exposes life which, as the biblical James has written, is "a mist that appears for a little while and then vanishes" (James 4:14). Yet these lives, pooled together with all of their unexpected twists and turns, give purpose and meaning to the city if we have eyes to see.

These books help us "read" the city. Each volume will share stories from a particular city, highlighting the unexpected twists and turns. They will provide a bibliography so you can dive deeper into the stories that catch your attention. They also provide a list of key sites so that you can follow your inspiration, creating "pilgrimages" to the actual setting of these stories. I encourage you to read a number of volumes in the series, from cities both near and far. Let them stir your imagination and teach you their wisdom for daily living.

One morning, as I was walking in my own city of Los Angeles, I became aware of the conversations of those who walked past me. They were all sharing stories of the joys and sorrows of being human. Later, as I had a coffee in a local cafe, I overheard more stories. Two people telling stories at a nearby table. Another man, near the door, telling a story to someone on the other end of the phone. A woman with her lap top, telling a story with rapid-fire typing, before e-mailing it to a friend.

How we love stories! We seem to need stories like we need air. My hope is that this series will add many stories to our repertoire; stories that will inspire us to think in new and constructive ways. Stories that we will share with others so that they, too, can discover more wisdom for their everyday lives.

Randy Lovejoy

Author's Introduction to La La Land

Ostriches were popular in late 19th century Los Angeles.

"Los Angeles is probably one of the most interesting spots on the face of the earth. Someone should write a book about it; an honest-to-goodness book, not a mere booster pamphlet....[1]"

-Louis Adamic

I tend to inhabit the margins. This probably explains why my wife and I raised our two sons in the middle of urban Los Angeles. "Tilt the country on one end and everything loose will slide into Los Angeles," Will Rogers once said. If California is on the margins of the United States, Los Angeles is on the margins of the margins. I have lived on this margin for more than twenty years.

Whether or not the stereotype of Los Angeles is true, I am certain that I came by this habit of living "off center" in my formative years. Born a Texan among generations of Texans, I spent part of elementary school in Sydney, Australia and most of high school in London, England. Since then I have lived in Mexico, Honduras, Mozambique and Zimbabwe. I have lived my life with friends and neighbors who saw life from a very different perspective than I did. My story as an American was on the margins of their story. Their story, as Brits and Aussies, as Mexicans, Hondurans, Mozambicans and Zimbabweans was on the margin of my story. I grew to love the challenge and adventure of living life on the margins.

My Christian faith only deepened this habit. When I chose to go deeper into my inherited faith I was drawn again to the margins. Though appropriated by Western culture in the last few centuries, Christianity, at its heart, is a non-Western religion. The Bible was first developed by Israelites and then by Jewish and Gentile Christians in their native Hebrew, Aramaic, and Greek. My Western view of reality was only "grafted in" to the narrative of the Scriptures after the climax in Jesus Christ. This story transcends all of the identity markers I use to determine my social location as a white, Anglo-Saxon, Protestant male. It places us all on common ground, with our perception of reality constantly critiqued and challenged by a faith in which there is neither Jew nor Greek, slave nor free, male nor female.

How, then, is a Western Christian living on the margins supposed to seek a greater understanding of Christianity in Los Angeles? By developing the story from his or her own point of view; recognizing that this is only one of many perspectives that are critical to the story. This prepares the way for listening to the stories of people living on the margins of our story. They have their own stories in which they are front and center. Only then can we achieve our goal: not to promote people on the margins of our story to the center of our story, but to engage them in a dialogue which respects their story. By allowing their story to impact and shape the very telling of our own.

This story of Christianity in Los Angeles is written as a supplement to the stories that have been written before (see bibliography for some of the stories resourced for this book). My hope is that this story will then be supplemented by other authors who live in different parts of the city, at other socio-economic levels, and from different communities of faith in the city. In this way a dialogue can develop between us on the margins where our stories overlap. Together we will find these margins to be a place of meeting, a gathering where we can look at the commonalities and differences of our stories. We might even share in the formation of a "congregation" gathered to enhance, correct and transform the way we understand and live out our lives in this city. If this occurs I will have achieved my heart-felt goal: to write a "real book" about Christianity in Los Angeles and not, as Adamic put it, "a mere booster pamphlet" for my particular point of view.

Randy Lovejoy

Los Angeles

www.randylovejoy.com

twitter: @revrandylovejoy

facebook: /revrandylovejoy

instagram: @randy.lovejoy

Lovejoy

Chapter 1

In the Beginning . . .

We have a tradition which points, indeed, to the vicinity of Los Angeles, the City of Angels, as the site of the very Paradise, and the graves are actually shown of Adam and Eve, father and mother of man, and (through some error, doubtless, since it is disputed that he died) of the serpent also. [1] *-The Health Seekers of Southern California, 1879-1900*

History can be as dry as dust. History in Los Angeles even more so. For Los Angeles is thought, even by Angelenos, to be a city built on a desert. But this is a myth. "El Pueblo de Nuestra Señora la Reina de los Ángeles sobre el Río Porciúncula" as the city was once called, is officially classified as a Mediterranean climate; wonderful for succulents and perfect for Christianity, given the soil in which the church first took root.[2] "L.A. as desert" is just one of many fruitful dreams, stories and legends which have been a part of this city since its founding.

An early Shoshonean creation story, for example, describes their journey to the region as one in which, ". . . the earth grew ever southward and the people followed."[3] It assigns the camp of the "first people" to a place in the Cajon Pass, a little over 60 miles north of downtown Los Angeles, when the earth was "still soft."[4]

Early California Facing South

In the sixteenth century, a different dream drew the Spanish to "Alta California." Their dream of a new sea route which would make their travel quicker and their trade more profitable was nourished by Garci Rodriguez De Montalvo's popular romance novel, *The Labors of the Very Brave Knight Esplandia,* published in 1510. "I will tell you that on the right-hand side of the Indies there was an island called California, which was very close to the region of earthly paradise."[5] This novel of chivalry and adventure gave rise to the idea that the region which now includes L.A. hid the entrance to a waterway which would make trade with Asia much less demanding. The Spanish colonial government took this dream seriously enough to send out Spanish explorers to find it.

Still another group of stories would have influence on both the Spanish and the Native Americans who would make first contact in this region. These stories featured a "woman in blue." Here is one example:

> It was...so many years ago that no man can count them. The chief of the Papago people was very old. He loved the son of his son, who one day would be chief; and he loved the boy the more for the reason that the boy's father, who was the old chief's son, was dead. But this boy lay now very sick in the lodge of his mother, and for two days the people of the village

had made prayers to their gods to spare the boy's life. But these prayers did not help, nor was the magic of the medicine man of any avail. ...the men and women of the village, having partaken of their evening meal, were sitting about the fire in the plaza, but the children were all in their lodges and asleep. All were silent and heavy of spirit because of the sickness that lay upon the chief's son . . . There came a flash of white light so bright that everyone was blinded by it, and when sight came slowly back to their eyes, they saw standing before them a young woman, clothed in strange robes of blue, and, my brother, she was of a beauty like to that of the full moon rising over the quiet waters.[6]

The theme of this mysterious woman in blue, also known as "Madre Maria," was most common among the people "of part Indian blood" around San Antonio, Texas. But it was found among tribes all the way to California. In 1921 Robert Sturmberg reported that "In...California, the trace of Madre Maria is found in numerous legends and beautiful folklore."[7]

These stories can be traced back, surprisingly enough, to a birth in the Spanish city of Agreda. Maria Coronel y de Arana was born on April 2, 1602 to Catalina de Arana and Francisco Coronel, a Jewish convert to Roman Catholicism. Though Maria would never travel to California she would have a major impact on both Native American and Spanish Catholic dreams in our region and beyond. As one author put it, Maria "...participated vicariously but effectively in the exploration of the Southwest."[8]

Maria de Agreda

From her early years, Maria had visions in which she experienced God instructing her about the sinfulness of the world. While in prayer she would enter into a trance. During this time, she would experience her soul going on a journey and then returning. This experience is not unlike the state that shamans in many native cultures experience except that she claimed to travel, not to the supernatural world, but to another part of the planet. This experience is known as bi-location.

In her account of these experiences, titled, "Face of the Earth," Maria describes how God moved her from broader visions of the universe to detailed visits to the land north of Mexico.

> 'It is densely populated,' she wrote, 'though I do not know if I should say by humans or animals; they seem more beasts than people and rational beings, though I can state that they are because while I was marveling that they could be, an angel said to me, 'Yes, they are, and they have a soul like yours.'[9]

This description of Native peoples is far more generous than those of many of the Spanish conquistadors of the day, some of whom refused to believe that the Native Americans had souls at all. Maria's vision, however, was strongly influenced by a Christian belief in the sanctity of all human life. The angel's description continues, "You will notice, dear soul that this group of people is so brutish that they do not realize that they are superior to the animals and they think they are all the same."[10] Maria's response to this vision again shows

24

how Christianity has shaped her perceptions beyond the cultural narrative of her day. She wrote: "Oh! How I wish I could set right and show the light to everyone who is without it so that they might know the Father of lights." Then, in an echo of Isaiah 6:8, Maria says, "Here am I, willing to die a thousand deaths for this cause."[11]

Whether she actually visited this region by bi-location is, of course, controversial. Maria reported that between 1620 and 1623 she was often transported by the aid of the angels to the settlement of a people called the Jumanos. Amazingly Franciscan Father Friar Juan de Salas would visit this very tribe in 1629.[12] Their folklore seems to provide evidence that she did in fact visit them. But there is another explanation.

Maria's confessor was an old priest with "a keen enthusiasm for extravagantly marvelous cases in religious life."[13] After hearing Maria tell of her experiences of bi-location, he sent a letter to Alonso de Benavides, the director of the Franciscan missions in New Mexico, asking him to investigate whether the Indians knew anything about Maria. At the time Benavides was trying to get a budgetary increase for the Franciscan work in the region, support for the creation of a new diocese of New Mexico, and, at the same time, fend off criticism of mass baptisms of Indians with little knowledge of Christianity at the missions. His accounts of Maria's bi-location experiences described her ministry as a preparation for the work of the missionaries by teaching the Gospel to the Indians and preparing them for their arrival. The Indians were ready, he argued, because Maria had already prepared them. These letters helped Benavides achieve his goals. He did get an increase in Spanish trade, protection and curiosity in the region. Some see these letters as the source of the legends of the lady in blue among the Native Americans.

Another scholar describes this kind of historical process as being "caught up and guided by a fusion of practical material interests and archetypal elements of myth --taken from one culture but adapted to the other to meet the needs of the circumstances."[14] "If we were to apply that approach to the bilocation we would not talk about lies, he writes, but about the powerful role of the imagination in both Benavides' and the Jumanos' reaction to the news of what the nun had told her confessor."[15] This process has also been documented among Spanish explorers. It seems that they included Indian mythology in their reports to other Spaniards justifying their request for another expedition.[16]

Whether Maria ever physically set foot in California or not, her visions had their impact. Her bi-location stories inspired a generation of Catholic missionaries to go the Alta California for the sake of their faith, including a Franciscan missionary named Junipero Serra. Serra, a Franciscan who played a critical role in California's missions, was heavily influenced by the theology of Dante's *Inferno*.[17] This vision of hell, with its circles of terror, developed into a passion to take the gospel to those who were forever lost unless they heard and received the message of Christ. This sense of responsibility was focused and directed by Maria's visions. For Junipero Serra, Maria's descriptions of the Native Americans who had not heard of Christ became a calling worthy of laying down one's life. He left the comfort of Europe to go the regions above Mexico and help the indigenous people escape the inferno which Serra himself had avoided through believing the gospel of Jesus Christ. Maria's influence in Serra's mission surfaces in a story written by Father Palou, a companion of Serra's:

> They all concurred in the choice of this spot for settlement; where upon the Venerable Father (Serra) ordered the mules to be unloaded and the bells hung from the branch of a tree. As soon as they could be rung, the servant of God began to sound them in a merry peal and to shout as if enraptured: 'Come you pagans; come, come to the Holy Church; come, come to receive the Faith of Jesus Christ.' One of the two Fathers who had been assigned by the president, Father Fray

Miguel Pieras, seeing this skeptically said to him: 'Why do you tire yourself here if this is not to be the spot where the church is to be built? Nor is there a single pagan anywhere abouts. It is a waste of time to ring the bells.' 'Father,' answered Fray Junipero, 'allow my overflowing heart to express itself. Would that this bell were heard throughout the world, as the Venerable Mother Sister Mary of Agreda desired it, or at least, that it were heard by every pagan who inhabits this sierra.'[18]

These stories of the lady in blue were cherished and remembered by a number of Native American peoples. The Papago legend, quoted above, continues:

All were filled with fear and were unable to speak or move. Then the young woman spoke to them, and bade them have no fear, but to listen to her words. There upon she told them of a new god, whereof they had not known before, and who was not like to any of their gods, but chief of them all. For a long time she spoke, and her tongue was like to the music of a mountain stream to the ears of a very thirsty man.[19]

These three stories are important archetypes for present day Los Angeles. For this city is a city of dreams. The dreams develop elsewhere. But then the dreamers are drawn to L.A. to pursue them. And there is a third motif which, for obvious reasons, remains hidden. The City of Angels, the city of dreams, makes no promise that the dreams pursued here will be fulfilled.

The Native American creation stories, for example, express a longing for a virgin land which these people could call their own. Archaeological evidence shows that the Tongva, a branch of the Shoshone nation that inhabited this region and made first contact with the Spanish, did make their home here for more than 3 millennia. But it also shows that this was not a virgin land. An ancient milling station was discovered recently, at the base of foothills near the city of Azusa in Los Angeles County, about two-thirds of the way between the Cajon Pass and Los Angeles. The site was in use some 8,000 years ago, pre-dating the arrival of the Tongva. Archeological records show that Native American habitation of the California coast goes back some 13,000 years. But the story of the earliest Native Americans in this area is shrouded in pre-history. The only clues to their existence are artifacts like the milling station and an unproven linguistic theory among scholars.[20] The Tongva moved into the area from Nevada about 3,500 years ago and displaced the previous tribe, only to be displaced themselves after the arrival of the Spanish.

A Shoshonean of the San Jacinto Mountains

The Spanish dreamed of a land they called California, which would grant them a short cut to Asia with better opportunities to trade. The pursuit of this dream expanded their empire into Alta California. This dream was tenacious. It only died after the area had been fully explored. They never found the short cut they were searching for.

The Spanish Catholic dream for the area wasn't fulfilled either. Maria de Agreda envisioned the Native Americans freed from damnation by the gospel of Jesus Christ, a vision which inspired the Spanish missions to the region. But as early as 1927 Edward Wicher was able to write, "Today it is impossible to find traces of religious influence exercised by the Padres among the Indians of the State of California."[21] And in 1938, 17 years after

Sturmberg's book on the legends of the Lady in Blue among the Native Americans, Hallenback and Williams, co-authors of *Legends of the Southwest* could find no trace of these stories in Southern California.[22]

Huntington Gardens, in Los Angeles County, hosts one of the largest congregations of succulents in the entire world. The "Desert Garden" features more than 2,000 varieties of succulents, ranging from the beautiful to the bizarre, and bearing names like Cacti, Agave, Sedum, and Echeveria. This huge mosaic of succulents shares a common physiological adaptation which allows them to thrive, not only in the desert, but also in the Mediterranean ecosystems on which the city of L.A. is built.

Perhaps this succulent garden in the Huntington is a sort of parable about life in Los Angeles. L.A. is indeed a city of dreams; dreams inspired in myriad places and brought to the city by a vast multitude of peoples. They are drawn here by the idea that maybe, just maybe, this will be the city where their dreams will come true. And though there is no guarantee that these dreams will be fulfilled, it is the adaptation required by the gap between the dreams pursued and the reality achieved which produces the creative experiments for which Los Angeles is known.

Like the desert garden in the Huntington, the City of Angels stimulates innovation and experimentation as dreamers come and pursue their passion; a fantastical flowering for all to see.

29

Lovejoy

Chapter 2

California Dreamin'

All the leaves are brown,

And the sky is grey

I've been for a walk

on a winter's day

I'd be safe and warm

If I was in L.A.

California dreamin'

On such a winter's day.

-The Mamas and the Papas[1]

I'm not sure that anyone has grasped the essence of the city of Los Angeles. It isn't for a lack of trying. Aldous Huxley, Upton Sinclair, William Faulkner, and F. Scott Fitzgerald put their pen to paper in the attempt, as have Simone De Beauvoir, Joan Didion, Jan Morris, and Carol Musk. And this is just to name a few. You would think, with all this creative ability, that somebody would have captured it. But everyone seems to have their own take on the city based upon their own point of view. The essence of Los Angeles, it seems, is found in the eye of the beholder.

Some describe Los Angeles by means of its geography. The Pacific Ocean forms the southern and western boundaries, giving rise to the beach culture that is such a part of the city. Its northern and eastern boundaries are mountains: the foothills of the Santa Monica mountains and the San Gabriela.

Many of L.A.'s most beautiful homes are built on one of the numerous hills, canyons and valleys which also make up Los Angeles. Together the geography offers Angelenos a walk on the beach one day and hiking in the forest the next. All this surrounding a city which measures 469 square miles situated on a coastal plain 340 feet above sea level.

Small wonder that Los Angeles has long been the destination of people who seek healthier living. This trend goes back to its early days. Louis Adamic, a Slovenian immigrant, writer, and labor activist, wrote in 1926, "Health is a big thing in Los Angeles. Most people come here to be sun-kissed and made well, and so healing is one of the big industries in town. Besides thousands of more or less regular doctors, there are in Los Angeles no end of chiropractors, osteopaths, "drugless physicians," faith-healers, health lecturers, manufacturers and salesmen of all sorts of health "stabilizers" and "normalizers," psychoanalysts, hypnotists, mesmerists, the glow-of-life mystics, astro-therapists, miracle men and women --in short, quacks and charlatans of all descriptions."[2] One health movement in 1929 was led by nutritionist and pioneer of America's wellness movement, Paul Bragg. Bragg urged deep breathing, water fasts, organic food, juicing and exercise, promising that every human could live to 120 years of age if they would follow his regime. He died decades short of this claim, but Jack LaLanne once said that Bragg had saved his life when he attended a Bragg Crusade in Oakland, CA at the age of 15. LaLanne went on to become the "Godfather of Fitness" calling physical culture and nutrition "the salvation of America."[3]

L.A. has also been described in other ways; according to its industry and citizenry, for example. The main industries in the city have shifted multiple times over the life of Los Angeles, from foraging among the Native Americans, to farming at the Spanish Missions, from vast cattle ranchos and large-scale agriculture, to oil and real estate. Today L.A. is often described as a center of international trade and banking, of manufacturing, and tourism; not to mention the entertainment industry. The city can also be described by her population. Los Angeles is the second largest city in the United States and home to one of the most multiethnic urban areas in the United States.

Each of these descriptions goes some distance in describing some part of Los Angeles. But none of them capture its particular quality as a city.

Perhaps part of the difficulty has to do with the City of Dream's peculiar approach to history. While doing research for this book in the Caravan Book Store in downtown Los Angeles, I asked the owner, Leonard Bernstein, why it was so challenging to find books on the history of this city. He told me, with the wisdom of his more than 40 years as proprietor of the store, that L.A. doesn't reflect on the past. The city, he said, is always moving on to the next thing.

For example, when the ancient mill station near Azusa mentioned in the last chapter was discovered, it did not hinder the dreams of the real estate developers who found it. New housing was built on the site and, though the artifacts were preserved, at the time of this writing it is unclear where they are being kept or how one might view them.

The site of the historic Wolfskill adobe is another example. This building, which played a key role in the development of orange agriculture in Los Angeles, was torn down to make way for the Southern Pacific's Arcade Station. As the railroad continued to transform the city, that station was demolished so that the Central Depot could better serve rail passengers. With the development of the automobile and freeway system as public transportation of choice in L.A., the Central Depot was demolished and replaced by a meat packing plant.[4] Dream replaces dream, which replaces dream.

Ryan Holiday wrote, "LA is a city that continually obscures its own history and forgets what it has going for it. So it's no wonder that 'getting it' is so difficult."[5]

But this hasn't stopped multitudes of creative artists from trying to capture the essence of the city.

Pershing Square, in downtown Los Angeles, has as good of a claim as any to be the center of the city. It is home to a statue bearing the description from 1946 by Carey Mc Williams, long time L.A. resident and 20-year editor of *The Nation Magazine*:

> In the center of the park, a little self-conscious of my evening clothes, I stopped to watch a typical Pershing Square divertissement: an aged and frowsy blonde, skirts held high above her knees, cheered by a crowd of grimacing and leering old goats, was singing a gospel hymn as she danced gaily around the fountain. Then it suddenly occurred to me that in all the world there neither was, nor would there ever be, another place like this city of Angels...here indeed was the place for me, a ring side seat at the circus.[6]

Decades earlier in his 1915 book *The Art of the Motion Picture*, Poet Vachel Lindsay, looks to the burgeoning movie industry in L.A. and describes the city as a kind of Athens of the modern age.[7]

By contrast, Bertold Brecht, the poet and playwright who escaped Nazi Germany and lived and wrote in Los Angeles for 6 years, expressed a more pessimistic take on the city:

Alas, the lovely garden, placed high above the coast

Is built on crumbling rock. Landslides

Drag parts of it into the depths without warning. Seemingly

There is not much time left in which to complete it.[8]

Lindsay looked at Los Angeles and saw a budding, cultured civilization. Brecht saw a garden which might never come to fruition. McWilliams, writing just a few years after Brecht, saw a circus. And when David Reid looked at the city more recently, in 1992, he used still another metaphor. Los Angeles is, in his words:

> a human laboratory of racial, ethnic and cultural diversity that stretches from the Downtown skyscrapers to the teaming apartments of mid-Wilshire; from the drug infested gang turf of Pico and Vermont on the south to the million-dollar hillside homes abutting Griffith Park on the north.[9]

Who is right? Is Los Angeles the site of a budding, cultured civilization or is it a budding but doomed garden? Is it a circus or is it a laboratory? Or is it one of a hundred other depictions in literature, film and song? What is Los Angeles? In a sense, all of them. For the peculiar, unorganized, yet strongly united dream of many Angelinos to re-create themselves has formed a city which allows its inhabitants the individual freedom, not only to experience the city in their own way, but also to describe that personal experience as if it were a definitive description of the city as a whole. This seems to be part of the inner workings of the pursuit of dreams in L.A.; a theme that threads through all of the descriptions and experiences of the city.

Take the story of a businessman like Henry C. Jensen, for example. Jensen was a German immigrant to the United States, one of many who arrived in Los Angeles in the 1880's to build it into a metropolis. In 1821 L.A. was a small town in the Alta California region of the Republic of Mexico with a population of under one thousand. In 1850 it became a part of the new

35

American state of California having grown to a population of 1,610. When the railroads arrived, first from San Francisco in 1876, and then from a whole variety of locations via the Atchison, Topeka, and Santa Fe railways in 1886, Los Angeles grew dramatically to 50,000 people. Jensen arrived right in the middle of this growth, with a dream of success through the brick making business.

By 1902 Jensen's success, like the city, was expanding. His knowledge of brickworks, developed earlier in Illinois, Utah and Oregon, enabled him to build his personal fortune in alignment with the growth of the city. He then expanded into real estate. He bought more than 16 acres of land and successfully developed it. In 1912 the community now known as Harvard Heights was born. Then he turned his sights toward Hollywood.

Two years previous, in 1910, Hollywood had been annexed to become the center of a new industry in Los Angeles. "Seeking refuge from Thomas Edison's patent enforcers[10] and relishing the climate, among other factors, the motion picture industry slowly migrated west from New York to create a vast entertainment factory by the 1920's."[11] In 1912 Jensen built a $35,000 domed movie palace for the Globe Theater Company. Two years later he built Glendale's first movie theater, the Pacific Grand on Brand Boulevard not far from the present-day Glendale Galleria and the Americana at Brand.

Then, in 1924 Jensen built a recreation center in Echo Park. It was one of the first buildings in Los Angeles to combine entertainment with retail and apartments. Memorialized by a 17ft x 28ft incandescent sign depicting a bowler throwing a strike, a bowling alley was at the center of the original building. The 50,000 square foot structure, designed by architect E.B. Meinardus, included 46 apartments and was built for $200,000. There were critics of his industrial success in his day as well as ours.[12] But for Henry Jensen, at this time in his life, Los Angeles was the city of his dreams.

Jensen's Recreation Center

Another businessman whose personal dream for success was fulfilled in L.A. was the Welsh immigrant and mining expert G.J. Griffith. Griffith became even wealthier than Jensen. His success enabled him, in 1882, to purchase about 4,000 acres of the Rancho Los Feliz Mexican land grant. In 1896 he and his wife presented 3,015 acres of it to the city of Los Angeles as a Christmas present. Griffith said, "I consider it my obligation to make Los Angeles a happy, cleaner, and finer city. It must be a place of rest and relaxation for the masses, a resort for the rank and file, for the plain people. I wish to pay my debt of duty in this way to the community in which I have prospered."[13] Today this "Christmas gift" constitutes the majority of Griffith Park, one of the largest urban parks in the United States.

The experience of these men, and others like them, grew into a view of the L.A. as the place to find personal success. The entertainment industry played no small part in the development and maintenance of this image. A 1923 film review of the movie *Hollywood* by critic Janet Garza says this: "The usual tale of a pretty girl from the sticks trying to break into movies..."[14] As Jim Heimann put it, "Hollywood monopolized the world's imagination, and the movie mystique drew thousands of fans to L.A. to pursue that dream, recasting their lives and discarding their past--an allure that continues right up to today."[15]

This theme received another boost in the next generation with the dream of Michelle and John Phillips. In 1963 they wrote the hit song, "California Dreamin." The lyrics of the song highlight our theme, but with a particular emphasis on the pull Los Angeles has on people to leave their home to pursue that dream.

Michelle was living in New York with John, but homesick for Los Angeles, thus the first verse of the song:

> All the leaves are brown,
> And the sky is grey
> I've been for a walk
> on a winter's day
> I'd be safe and warm
> If I was in L.A.
> California dreamin'
> On such a winter's day.

The second verse, however, is more reflective of John Phillips. Michelle enjoyed visiting St. Patrick's Cathedral in New York. John did not as it reminded him of his negative parochial school experience, reflected in this next verse.

> Stepped into a church I passed on the way
> Well, I got down on my knees
> and I pretend to pray
> you know the preacher like the cold
> He know I'm gonna stay

He didn't like the verse but couldn't think of anything else. So it stayed. The next verse moves the song to a decision point. The dream is present, but will it be followed? The final verse only deepens this struggle by repeating the first verse and then replacing the last two lines in a way which highlights the challenge of following the dream.

> All the leaves are brown
> And the sky is grey
> I've been for a walk
> On a winter's day
> If I didn't tell her
> I could leave today

The dream of Walt Disney has also played its part in deepening this image of L.A. as the city of dreams. In the same year as Janet Garza's movie review, Disney moved from Chicago to Los Angeles and achieved considerable success in animation. The fulfillment of this dream allowed the development of an even greater dream: a theme park. The idea developed through visits to Griffith Park with his daughters. Heavily influenced by Tivoli Gardens in Copenhagen he purchased a large plot of land in Anaheim to develop a park described in an editorial in the New York Times as having "tastefully combined some of the pleasant things of yesterday with fantasy and dreams of tomorrow."[16] The park opened in 1955 and continues today. In 2015 the average daily attendance was estimated at 44,000. Among the branding slogans of Disneyland are "Where dreams come true."

But, as we have seen, there is no guarantee that the dreams brought to Los Angeles will come true. And if they do come true there is no promise that they will be fulfilling. The City of Dreams is, in this sense, a case study in the human condition. Yuval Noah Harari, in his book, *Homo Deus* writes, "It appears that our happiness bangs against some mysterious glass ceiling that does not allow it to grow despite all of our unprecedented accomplishments."[17] This is true in Los Angeles. People are drawn here to seek their dreams, but inevitably those people hit a wall. Jensen and Griffith's lives are cases in point.

When the Great Depression hit the United States in the 1930's, the optimism which had developed over three decades of growth in Los Angeles was lost. The economy stagnated and Jensen lost his fortune. The recreation center and its incandescent sign flashing the bright hope of Jensen's dreams were shut down. The sign wouldn't be turned on again for another 60 years.

Jensen's dream turned darker, more akin to a nightmare. In 1936 while Jensen was on vacation with his wife and his son Walter, "Walter went fishing for swordfish 20 feet off the coast of Catalina Island. The sea was rough and Walter slipped and fell into the churning sea. Captain George Gibson and his assistant attempted to pull Walter aboard, but his great weight made this difficult. He was unconscious by the time he was retrieved from the water. Three hours later, after an inhalator failed to revive him, Walter was pronounced dead."[18]

Jensen retreated from life after his son's death. No new projects were announced. No new buildings to lease. The *L.A. Times* makes no further mention of Henry C. Jensen until his death eight years later. He was buried next to his son "with full Masonic rights in the Rosedale Cemetery, surrounded by the houses he had constructed forty years before."[19]

Griffith's dream also became a nightmare. Seven years after he so generously gifted the acreage for the park which still bears his name, Griffith shot his wife point blank in their hotel room while vacationing in Santa Monica. Although she survived, she was left disfigured and lost her right eye. During the ensuing trial it was revealed that Griffith was an alcoholic who suffered paranoid delusions. He was sentenced to two years in San Quentin. He died in 1919, after serving his time and was interred at the Hollywood Forever Cemetery.[20] The bulk of his $1.5 million estate was used to build the Greek Theater and the Griffith Park Observatory, both in Griffith Park.

Griffith Park with over 53 miles of trails.

The dark side of the dream fulfilled surfaces in the life of Raymond Chandler as well. Chandler, an American novelist and screenwriter whose work was so successful that his literary genre became almost synonymous with Los Angeles, moved to the city with his mother in 1913. By 1931 Chandler had worked his way up to vice president of the Dabney Oil Syndicate. After just one year in the position, however, alcoholism, absenteeism, promiscuity with female employees, and threatened suicides cost him his job.

He found success again in L.A. This time as a detective fiction writer. From 1940-1953 Chandler wrote a series of novels considered masterpieces: *Farewell, My Lovely* (1940), *The Little Sister* (1949), and *The Long Goodbye* (1953). *The Long Goodbye* was praised in an anthology of American crime stories as " . . . arguably the first book since Hammett's *The Glass Key*, published more than twenty years earlier, to qualify as a serious and significant mainstream novel that just happened to possess elements of mystery."[21] When his books were made into films, Phillip Marlowe, the protagonist of his novels, was played by screen legend Humphrey Bogart. To this day, Chandler is considered the founder of a distinctive style of detective fiction along with authors like Dashell Hammett.

But then his dream took an "L.A. turn." In 1954 Chandler was thrown into a tailspin by the death of his wife after a long illness. Loneliness and clinical depression made his drinking worse. His writing was affected. In 1955 he tried to commit suicide. He died in La Jolla in 1959.

The number of people who have experienced what I call the "L.A. turn" are legion. Fatty Arbuckle, the famous silent film artist who mentored Charlie Chaplin and discovered Buster Keaton and Bob Hope, signed a contract with Paramount in 1920 for $1,000,000 (the equivalent of $13,000,000 in 2016). Over the next two years, however, he featured more prominently in real life than film. Arbuckle was a defendant in a rape and manslaughter case. Though the case resulted in his eventual acquittal, it overshadowed his career for the rest of his life. Arbuckle died of a heart attack at age 46. His was just one of many tragic endings to an L.A. dream.

Marilyn Monroe was died of a barbiturate overdose in her home on August 5, 1962. Comedian Lenny Bruce committed suicide in 1966. Freddie Prinze also died of suicide in 1977. The list goes on: John Belushi in 1982, Margaux Hemingway in 1996, Brian Keith in 1997, David Foster Wallace in 2008, Tony Scott in 2012, Chester Bennington in 2017. The fulfillment of their dreams in Los Angeles was not enough.

In 1985 Stevie Wonder released a song describing this aspect of life in L.A. The final verse of the song, "The Land of La-La" reads:

You might get everything you want

But not want everything you get

Being in la la land is like nowhere else

Living in the land, one hell of a land, a land full of lost angels

Movie stars and great big cars and Perrier and fun all day

And that's enough to make anybody go wild

In the land of la la

He's a big boy now, she's a strong girl

But only the strong can survive

Living in the land of la la

Stories like Chandler's, Arbuckle's and so many others make sense of the contrast between the year-round sunshine in a coastal city between the mountains and the sea and the cynical descriptions of L.A., so common among professional writers. As Carolyn Sees puts it in *Golden Days*, "Southern California bespeaks alienation. The West Coast is the end of the road for the American Dream. We're up against a blank wall out here, and we can't go any farther. So, even if you get what you want, then what? There is no out, you're here. It looks good, but that's it.[22]

In spite of these stories, people continue to move to Los Angeles. And they define Los Angeles in their own way, as if their description were a description of the whole. Pico Iyer wrote, "In a city where myth-making is an industry, L.A.'s writers have often felt the need to resist imposed narratives, preferring to carve out their own version of reality, no matter how fragmentary."[23]

One theme, however, runs through all of the descriptions: L.A. as a city of dreams. Those dreams, as we said in the previous chapter, are pursued without guarantee of success. And, as we have seen in this chapter, there is no guarantee that, if successful, these dreams will be fulfilling. But there is still one more facet of this theme which will be seen in the next chapter. Above all of the unfulfilled and unfulfilling dreams in Los Angeles there is a story which seems to transcend it all.

Simone De Beauvoir's description of the city captures this transcendence. Looking beyond the cynicism of unfulfilled dreams she makes use of the language of her childhood Christian faith which, though rejected, still provided the imagination needed to see the city of Angels in all of its hope and sorrow:

> Los Angeles is beneath us, a huge, silent fairyland. The lights glitter as far as the eye can see. Between the red, green and white clusters, big worms slither noiselessly. Now I am not taken in by the mirage: I know that these are merely street lamps along the avenues, neon signs, and headlights. But mirage or no mirage, the lights keep glittering; they, too, are a truth. And perhaps they are even more when they express nothing but the naked presence of men. Men live here, and so the earth revolves in the quiet of the night with this shining wound in its side.[24]

Chapter 3

A Tale of Two Churches

A large gathering is expected to attend the ceremonies at Echo park this afternoon, when Rev. J. L. Griffin, the negro evangelist, will immerse a number of candidates. Permission has been granted Dr. Griffin to use the lake for the day...Dr. Griffin has a record of having baptized more than 8,000 converts.

-Los Angeles Herald, September 1907

The history of Christianity can be as dry as dust, Christianity in Los Angeles even more so. Just ask the early Protestant pastors who tried to gather people for worship in mid-1800s L.A. The town gathered. But not for church. As one newspaper reporter wrote in 1853: "An instance of the diversity of entertainment afforded to the public...take the following: On Tuesday of last week we had four weddings, two funerals, one street fight with knives, a lynch court, two men flogged, a serenade by a band, a fist fight and one man tossed in a blanket."[1] And yet this "vile little dump,"[2] as one nineteenth century pastor called Los Angeles, would be the backdrop to many expressions of the transcendence of the human spirit including our tale of two churches.

Our first story begins with the birth of a baby girl on October 15, 1818. On that date, Ms. Bridget "Biddy" Mason was born into slavery. Much of her history is unwritten, but we do know that she was owned by the Mason family, part of a cotton plantation in Hancock County, Georgia. Sometime between 1844 and the spring of 1848 she was purchased by Robert Mays Smith, a South Carolinian who had used his inheritance to start a new life in

Mississippi. While there, Smith converted to Mormonism, a conversion which caused his family to become embroiled in a wider persecution of Mormons in that state. As a result, he moved his family and possessions from Mississippi to Utah and then to California in search of a better life. They arrived in California on June 9, 1851 and eventually settled in Los Angeles.

In December of 1855 Smith was preparing to move again, this time to Texas. When the Los Angeles County Sheriff heard that slaves were going to be moved from California, a free state, to Texas, a slavery state, he gathered a posse and apprehended Smith's wagon train in Cajon Pass, California. After three days of deliberation, Los Angeles District Judge Benjamin Hayes handed down a ruling which freed Mason, citing California's 1850 constitutional prohibition of slavery. For the rest of her life, Biddy carried a certified court order stating her "freedom for life".

Benjamin Hayes

A February 2, 1856 article in the *Los Angeles Star* reported that "The plaintiffs claiming their freedom were discharged and have hired themselves in different families in the city." Biddy worked as a nanny and a nurse. She earned $2.50 a day, a good salary at that time for an African-American woman. After 10 years she had saved $250 which she used on November 28, 1866 to purchase property. That purchase made her one of the first African-American women to own property in Los Angeles. But Mason was just getting started. She purchased her first property on November 28, 1866. But Mason was just getting started. She built a clap board house for herself on the property which was on Spring Street between 3rd and 4th. She also built some small rental houses. Two years later, she purchased a second lot. Later, she built a commercial building on another plot of land, renting out the storerooms on the ground floor of the building. In the early 1890s the main financial district of Los Angeles had developed around her property. Biddy Mason became one of the wealthiest African-American women in the city.

Spring Street before 1884

Mason became a generous philanthropist. In response to one of the floods, which were common in Los Angeles at the time, she asked a grocer to feed any family who had lost their home. She would reimburse him. Needy people would line up in front of her home for assistance.[3] Biddy fed and sheltered the poor and visited prisoners in the local jail with gifts and aid. She was instrumental in founding a traveler's aid center for people in need of transit assistance as well as an elementary school for black children. Because of her kind and giving spirit, many called her Grandma Mason. She was known to say, again and again, "If you hold your hand closed, nothing good comes in."[4]

Her generosity also spread to the church. She hosted the first meeting of what would become the First African Methodist Episcopal Church of Los Angeles (F.A.M.E.) in her home on Spring Street. She also donated a property on Eighth and Towne Streets, which would become the site of the congregation's first church building in 1903.

Bridget "Biddy" Mason

The Apostle Paul once wrote that in Christ Jesus there is "neither Jew nor Gentile, neither slave nor free, nor is there male and female."[5] These words become reality in the life of Biddy Mason. Other African-Americans in the history of Los Angeles, like Biddy Mason, have also had to learn how to overcome social barriers or become defined by them. But such barriers did not always exist in the City of Angels.

People of African descent, long before they were called "African-Americans," played a key role in the city. When Los Angeles was first established in 1781, 26 of the original 46 settlers were black or mulatto.[6] In 1793 Juan Francisco Reyes, a settler of both African and Spanish heritage, was elected as the seventh Mayor of Los Angeles. Having been a member of the 1769 Portola expedition which included Father Junipero Serra (see chapter 6) he would also serve as Mayor until 1795.

Name	Age		Birthplace	Residence
Manuel Agugue	48		Mexico	LA county
Tomasa Agugue	35		Mexico	LA county
Margarita Balenzuela	2		California	LA county
Peter Biggs	35		Virginia	LA city
Josefa U. Chosofo	18		California	LA city
Malvina Conway	20		Kentucky	LA city
William Davis	27		Mississippi	LA city
Julia Douglass	45		Georgia	LA city
Lucy Evertsen (Mulatto)	6		Florida	LA city
Ignacio Fernandez	30		Guatemala	LA city
Becky Hardige	16		Arkansas	LA city
Susan Hardige	14		Alabama	LA city
Clarissa Holman	27		Tennessee	LA city
William Roldan	24		New York	LA city
Maria Ruddle	17		Missouri	LA city

(from the 1850 census of Los Angeles)

African-Americans in Los Angeles, likely an undercount.

Blacks and mulattoes in Los Angeles began to experience legal discrimination after California was handed over to the United States in 1848. Many white Southerners who came to California during the Gold Rush (1848-1855) brought racist attitudes and ideals with them.

Even after these social barriers developed, the African-American population continued to grow. By 1900, 2,131 African-Americans called L.A. home, the second largest African-American population in California. People of African heritage continued to play an important role, not only in this history of Los Angeles, but in the history of Christianity in Los Angeles. Take J.L. Griffin, for example. The story of Billy Graham's tent revival in Los Angeles in 1949 has been well-documented. But more than four decades earlier the *Los Angeles Herald* newspaper announced that a "negro evangelist" held tent meetings in the city.

J. L. GRIFFIN WILL OPEN REVIVAL

Negro Evangelist Will Address White People in Volunteers' Hall Tonight—Has Secured Tent for Meetings

J. L. Griffin, the negro evangelist, will preach to white people tonight in Volunteers' hall, First street, between Main and Los Angeles. Dr. Griffin, whose sobriquet, 'Sin Killer Griffin' and his song 'Get on the Gospel Chariot,' have made him famous in many states, is in Los Angeles to the purpose of carrying on evangelical work and to help the poor and unfortunate regardless of creed or race. After three months' work he has secured subscriptions sufficient to purchase a large tent, 300 chairs and an organ. The tent is situated at Ninth and Mateo streets, and here will be held large meetings every night, at which Dr. Griffin and others will speak.

Dr. Griffin is recommended by mayors of forty cities and the governors of many states. In connection with the evangelical work there has been organized a sewing circle. Dr. Griffin makes an appeal to charitable people for aid in his work and for supplies for the needy. His home address is 1323 Santa Fe Avenue.[7]

And then this follow up article on September 23, 1907:

A crowd of 2,000—the faithful and the doubters—gathered at Echo Park Lake as black evangelist the Rev. J.L. Griffin prepared to baptize five believers in the cold water. Children climbed in the trees to get a better view, while other people trolled in rowboats to watch.

The rite was supposed to begin at 4 p.m., but several of the people were delayed and Griffin, who had been holding tent revival meetings in Los Angeles all summer, addressed the increasingly impatient throng.

'Some of you colored men have criticized me because I am friendly with white people,' Griffin said.' 'I tell you the Lord loves us all, white or black. We are on the watch for sanctification and separation.'

'What is separation, Mr. Preacher?' a skeptic yelled.

'I'll tell you what separation means for you, my friend," Griffin replied. "It means separation from your devilment, that's what.'

Born in the days of slavery, Griffin, 48, of Dallas, was an imposing, powerful man who began preaching at an early age. In 1868, he went to live on a Louisiana farm and while there, learned to read from an old green-backed *Webster's Speller*.

'Then I read the Testament, lots of times, from cover to cover, and some of the colored folks, they heard me talk about it. In them days the big preachers came into the country to preach sometimes and get a good collection. Finally some of the folks asked why I don't preach and I did; I began at 9 years old.'

Griffin frequently engaged the congregation in his sermons:

'You, Sam, you always done shot craps, didn't you?'

'Yes, sir.'

'You going to do it anymore?'

'Lord, no sir.'

A small disrobing tent was erected in the park. Annie Childs was the first to come forth in a white robe and a white handkerchief over her head. The article described the scene: "She seemed unconscious of the onlookers and broke into an ecstatic song as she walked to the water's edge."

J. L. Griffin in Echo Park, 1907

The five believers to be baptized on this day were multiethnic: three black, one white and one Latino. The crowd hushed as Child's face dipped below the surface of the lake. Again quoting the times:

> In an instant she reappeared, spluttering and sobbing in excitement. Once out of the lake, she went into a spasm. Her garments, saturated with water, clung tightly to her slight figure. Her eyes were closed. Suddenly she began to cry and laugh and to shout religious phrases that gave evidence to the glory that was hers.

Several hecklers steered their rowboats near Griffin, but he cautioned them:

'You boys had better get away or I might give you a different kind of baptism.'

More recently, in 1931, Spencer Williams, of Amos and Andy fame, founded Lincoln Talking Pictures Company. In 1941 the movie, *The Blood of Jesus*, written and directed by Williams, was a major success. His other films included *Brother Martin: Servant of Jesus*, *Marchin' On*, *Go Down Death* and *Of One Blood*.[8]

In 1977, Dr. Cecil L. "Chip" Murray was assigned by the A.M.E. Bishop to F.A.M.E. Los Angeles. During the next 27 years, Dr. Murray led the church which Biddy Mason did so much to start. By the mid-20th century this congregation's membership would grow to 18,000, supporting more than 40 community programs through 13 corporations with an annual budget of more than $2,000,000. With an increased emphasis on social welfare under his watch, the church's membership grew from 250 to 18,000. In 1980 President George H.W. Bush named First A.M.E. the 177th point of light in the nation.

Our second story begins on the other side of the social barriers of Los Angeles. But like the story of the First A.M.E. and Biddy Mason, this story features a person who made their money in real estate in Los Angeles. Alvah Warren Ross' life is the story of an insider who steadily and courageously climbed the existing social ladder in pursuit of his dream to create a new economic center in Los Angeles. When his dream was fulfilled, that center became a region where houses of worship, including Immanuel Presbyterian Church, thrived.

In the early 1920s, Wilshire Boulevard, to the west of Western Avenue, was an unpaved oil road meandering through dairy farms and bean fields. But developer A.W. Ross looked on that dirt road and envisioned a commercial district to rival the commercial center which had flourished around Biddy Mason's first two properties. The distinctive feature of this new commercial district would be a focus, not on pedestrian traffic as in downtown Los Angeles, but on automobile traffic. Fellow businessmen who heard about Ross' dream would laugh and wish him luck, he told the *Los Angeles Times* in a 1939 retrospective. The project became known as "Ross' bean patch" and "Ross' folly." The arrival of the then popular Desmond's Department Store followed by Silverwood, Coulter's and the May Company transformed "Ross' folly" into what became the "Miracle Mile."

The Miracle Mile
Nathan Dumlao on Unsplash

The success of Ross' dream opened up all kinds of social innovation in Los Angeles and beyond. The Miracle Mile featured the first dedicated left turn lanes and the first timed traffic lights in the United States -- innovations designed to improve traffic flow for the would-be customers. Window displays were designed to draw the attention of potential shoppers driving through the Wilshire district. Ross' approach to urban development, which became known as "the linear downtown" model,[9] was used in the economic development of other cities around the United States.

Major businesses were not the only ones drawn to Ross' "bean patch." The Baptists, Unitarians, Episcopalians, Methodists, Presbyterians, and the Jewish community invested significantly in large church structures still present today on Wilshire Boulevard. None of these congregations were new congregations. St. James Episcopal started in 1911 moving once before its move to Wilshire Boulevard in 1926. It was also the third move in the 67 years for Wilshire Boulevard Temple since its founding. Immanuel Presbyterian moved from downtown to their present location on Wilshire Boulevard in 1929. By 1930 this section of L.A. was not only a commercial district rivaling downtown Los Angeles, but also a spiritual center of the city.

Immanuel Presbyterian Church on the Miracle Mile was the fruit of a story of persistence and courage going back to 1874. It was in that year that a Presbyterian "home missionary" cut out of the same cloth as A.W. Ross set his sights on the City of Angels. The Rev. James Fraser asked the Presbyterian Board of Home Mission for funding to support his efforts in Los Angeles. The Presbyterians had given up trying to establish a permanent Presbyterian congregation in the city after numerous failures. When Fraser asked for support, their skepticism remained. They replied to his request saying, "After all our failures we have no faith in Los Angeles. Work it out on your own faith, not ours." Fraser persevered. Eleven years later, First Presbyterian Church of Los Angeles had 2,600 members. The congregation would plant a half-dozen new Presbyterian Churches in Los Angeles, one of which was Immanuel.

In 1888, the Pastor of 1st Presbyterian Church, William Chichester, felt called to reduce his salary and use the money to expand the congregations reach. He took 100 church members with him and started Immanuel Presbyterian Church at Tenth and Pearl Streets, an "a peach orchard" according to the Presbytery of Los Angeles. 35 years later Immanuel moved into a $1,000,000 French Gothic sanctuary on Wilshire Boulevard where it remains today.

The first church story embodies transcendence with a wonderful story of the First African-American congregation in Los Angeles built on land donated by a wealthy freed female slave. Our second story highlights the importance of immanence: faith aligning its ministry with economic and social development in the city. Both are important to and well represented in the history of Christianity in other cities.

In 1915, 62 years before the arrival of Dr. Murray, First A.M.E. suffered a schism. Popular pastor Napoleon P. Greggs was removed by the A.M.E. Bishop. Several members left First A.M.E. to join Greggs in the formation of the Independent Church of Christ. It was unclear if First A.M.E. would survive. But the Reverend J. Logan Craw took the pulpit and began to nurture the church back to health. The congregation stabilized. But the number of members at First A.M.E. would remain under 200 members for the next 50 years.

After Murray's pastorate from 1977-2004, F.A.M.E. again hit hard times. Dr. John Joseph Hunter succeeded Murray from 2005-2012. In 2012 the A.M.E. Bishop transferred First A.M.E. Pastor Dr. John Joseph Hunter to another congregation in San Francisco. That church refused to receive him. During his tenure at F.A.M.E. he had earned a reputation for free spending and was struggling with tax issues including a repayment of more than $100,000 spent on family vacations, clothes and jewelry. He was accused of "gross financial management" by church leaders and in 2009 was accused of forcing a former church employee into sexual service for four years, firing her when she finally refused to comply. Legal battles between the church and the pastor continued through 2014. Hunter was replaced at First A.M.E. by Rev. J. Edgar Boyd. His leadership seems, once again, to have moved the congregation past this struggle. Through the ups and downs of the past century, the church has continued to play an important role in Los Angeles.

The future of Immanuel Presbyterian Church is less clear. The Miracle Mile, which had proven so fruitful to her ministry, began to lose its luster. Other dreamers replaced A.W. Ross with new ideas. The linear model of urban development gave way to shopping malls with their hybrid driving/pedestrian focus. The venders who were the mainstay of the Miracle Mile moved out of the area. The economic growth which had played such a large part in the success of this region began to wane. The once magnificent buildings became shabby and unkempt. By the 1980s the Miracle Mile Residential Association described their own neighborhood as a slum. The churches of the Miracle Mile struggled as well. As the community changed, they lost the white-collar families who had supported their ministry financially. Their buildings became increasingly expensive to maintain. Most of the congregations simply didn't have the money they used to have.

Immanuel Presbyterian Church struggled to adapt to the change in ministry context. The pastoral leadership became uneven and problematic. In 1991 Immanuel Presbyterian made the headlines when Pastor Walker Railey was arrested in his church office. Railey had been hired as the church administrator after a high-profile fall from grace as Senior Pastor of the 6,000-member United Methodist Church in Dallas, Texas. His wife was found in the family home, strangled but still alive. Railey denied being involved. Suspicion was raised soon after when he left his comatose wife and two children to join his lover, Lucy Pappillon, who had a psychology practice in Beverly Hills.[10] He was in the position at Immanuel for less than a year before he was arrested and taken back to Texas to stand trial. The church accepted his resignation but suffered through bitter infighting over the incident.[11] This was the last thing that the congregation needed while struggling to survive the dramatic social and economic changes experienced by the Miracle Mile.

Recently there has been new hope of a revitalization in the Wilshire District, not with commerce, but with museums that have relocated to the area as the churches once did. Though this could revitalize the area, it is not enough to bring new life to the churches. First, unlike museums, churches cannot long survive as well-curated tributes to a 1920's commercial miracle. Second, the area continues its shift from white-collar to working class that cannot fund the increased cost of keeping up these ornate older buildings. But

Immanuel is trying. The Wilshire district is now 30% Black, 15% Asian and 10% Hispanic. Many are recent immigrants who are working hard to climb the economic ladder. In response, Immanuel Presbyterian Church self-describes as "a diverse, welcoming faith community located in the heart of Korea town and the Wilshire corridor." Their website continues: "We are a multicultural congregation, made up of many people from many nations, backgrounds and origins, United by our journey to seek God, do justice and share community."[12] The yet unanswered question is whether this will be enough to save Immanuel Presbyterian Church.

First A.M.E. has deep origins in the African-American experience in Western culture. The A.M.E.'s story traces back to The Right Reverend Richard Allen, a Methodist minister in Pennsylvania who, after obtaining his freedom from slavery, was part of a group of African-Americans who started the Free African Society. The purpose of the society, formed in 1787, was "to provide aid to newly freed blacks so that they could gather strength and develop leaders in the community."[13] Over time, Allen found his ministry with the Methodist church to be limiting. Like the Apostle Paul, he was starting new churches through an establishment that resisted the fruit of his labors. So, he took part in the formation of a new domination, the African Methodist Episcopal Church.

One would imagine that these roots would equip them to embrace recent immigrants, especially from Africa, more easily. But both First A.M.E. and Immanuel are expressions of Western Christianity. The A.M.E. has developed and refined its ecclesiology and religious practice in this context for over 200 years. Whether this African-American expression of Western Christianity will appeal to an African spirituality and theology, which does not share this particular experience of struggle, is an open question.

In his book, *A Tale of Two Cities*, author Charles Dickens details the turmoil and violence of social change in Paris and London. Underneath the description of chaos there is a belief that this will all, somehow, give way to a new and better city. The "Tale of Two Churches," like Dicken's *Tale of Two Cities*, reminds us that there is always hope of resurrection. The church can adapt and change with the city. As a matter of fact, it already has.

Lovejoy

Chapter 4

The Tabernacle in Los Angeles

Near the intersection of Short and Poppy Avenues in Compton, the branches of a massive sycamore spread over an apartment complex in a neighborhood where few large trees grow. Known as the Eagle Tree, it was one of the boundary markers of the giant Rancho San Pedro, a cattle ranch established in 1784 that sprawled over 75,000 acres from the Los Angeles River to the Pacific Ocean.[1]

Immanuel Presbyterian isn't the only church that is struggling to survive in Los Angeles. Many churches, especially those established before the 1950s, are in decline. Others have closed. For some this is a sign of Christianity's inevitable passing. Like the Eagle Tree it continues to exist, but only as a remnant of a more religious period in Western culture. But this view of Christianity in Los Angeles does not take into account the proven adaptability of this faith.

For millennia the Judeo-Christian faith has changed its structure in different contexts. Such adaptation goes back all the way to the wilderness wanderings of the Hebrews in the book of Exodus. In Exodus 24, when Moses met God on Mount Sinai to receive instructions on how to build the Tabernacle, we read that "the cloud covered it, and the glory of the Lord settled on Mount Sinai" (v. 15b). When the Tabernacle was completed, in Exodus 40:34, we read: "Then the cloud covered the tent of meeting, and the glory of the Lord filled the tabernacle." Three hundred years later, once the people of Israel gave up their nomadic life for a settled

Kingdom, the Tabernacle in the wilderness was superseded by the Temple in Jerusalem. When the Temple was completed in I Kings 8, we see a description of the transition in very similar language to Exodus, "When the priests withdrew from the Holy Place, the cloud filled the temple of the Lord. And the priests could not perform their service because of the cloud, for the glory of the Lord filled his temple" (v. 10-11). Generations later the worship of the Israelite God by Jewish and Gentile Christians transitions God's presence again to the person of Jesus. In John 1:14 we read, "The Word became flesh and made his dwelling among us. We have seen his glory, the glory of the one and only Son, who came from the Father, full of grace and truth." This language, literally that Jesus "pitched his tent" among us, echoes the language of the Tabernacle in the Hebrew Bible. The description continues: "We have seen his glory, the glory of the one and only Son, who came from the Father, full of grace and truth." As Dr. Raymond Brown writes, in his commentary on the gospel of John, "Jesus Christ is the new localization of God's presence on earth, and that Jesus is the replacement of the ancient Tabernacle.[2] D. Moody Smith agrees saying, "Jesus is the new temple or tabernacle, the new place where God manifests himself to man (sic), where his glory is beheld."[3]

Modern Western Christianity is only a more recent expression of this ability to transcend social change. Dr. Andrew Walls writes: "It took Christianity a long time to become a Western religion, let alone *the* Western religion. It did not begin as a Western religion...and it took many centuries to become thoroughly appropriated in Europe."[4] Christianity is adaptive. Christianity in Los Angeles is as well; like the succulents in the Desert Garden at the Huntington. It has already adapted and flourished at least three times in the Mediterranean climate of the City of Angels. There is every reason to believe it will do so again.

We can still find clues to these early chapters in the city and the church. Jan Morris said, in a 1976 *Rolling Stone* article,

In Los Angeles there are reminders of a long tradition. There is the very name of the city, and of its euphonious streets and suburbs--Alvarado, El Segundo, Pasadena, Cahuenga Boulevard. There is the pattern of its real estate, still recognizably descended from the Spanish and Mexican ranches of long ago.[5]

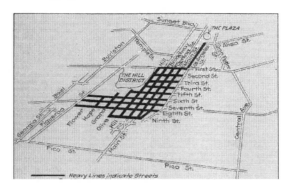

Los Angeles Map, 1908

One of those clues is the name "Pico." It shows up too often in Los Angeles to be an accident. There is Pico Boulevard, running more than 15 miles from the Pacific Ocean in Santa Monica to Central Avenue in Downtown. There is the city of Pico Rivera in Los Angeles County with over 60,000 inhabitants. There is the six-acre Pio Pico State Park in the city of Whittier. All three of these names lead us to a man whose life in L.A. provides a helpful structure for a broad view of Los Angeles. For Pio Pico, like Christianity, adapted and thrived across three major chapters of Los Angeles history; the Missions under the Spanish Monarchy, the Ranchos under Mexican rule and the burgeoning city under the governance of the United States.

Pio Pico was born at the Mission San Gabriel Arcangel on May 5, 1801 where his father served as corporal of the guard. This Mission and others like it, were the end result of an adaptation of Spanish Catholic Christianity and colonial culture. This was a complete way of life which shaped the lives of the Native Americans and the Spanish in this area for more than 60 years.

Mission San Gabriel

This system was the product of the Spanish dream, mentioned in the first chapter. As one historian put it,

> It was a great racial movement, inspired by ideas, romantic, religious and financial. The passion of it dominated for a while the entire population of Portugal and Spain . . . Seville, in particular, was so stripped of its inhabitants . . . that the city was left almost to the women.[6]

The goal of the Mission system was to incorporate Native Americans into Spanish society. The model for this system had been in development in other parts of the Americas for almost two centuries before it came to Southern California. So, when the Spanish arrived in Alta California, Jose de Galvez used this template to establish the standard frontier institutions. "They would set up military bases, or presidios, to protect their territory, while building missions to convert the natives to Christianity, creating a local workforce. Nearby civilian pueblos were planned, which would grow food to supply the needs of the colonists."[7] In this way the Spanish would create, from 1769-1833, 21 religious and military outposts in the Alta California.

This approach to Christian ministry in the Missions in Alta California had also been tested in other parts of New Spain. The Missions were centers of evangelization as well as agriculture and trade. "Their method of conversion was often a very simple one. It consisted of gifts of food and clothing by the Padres to the Indians, together with the promise of protection. No Indian was obliged to become converted, but having once accepted Christianity he was forbidden to leave the Mission."[8]

Once converted, the Indian Catholics were encouraged to live an orderly, settled existence, and were trained in agriculture and handicrafts. Their religious instruction focused on attendance at public worship, including daily morning and evening prayers. Their training in Catholic Christianity was extensive. It included the sign of the cross, the Lord's Prayer and the Hail Mary. They were taught the Apostle's Creed, the Confiteor (a prayer of confession), the act of contrition, the acts of faith, hope and charity, the Ten Commandments, the precepts of the Church, the seven sacraments (baptism, eucharist, confirmation, reconciliation, anointing of the sick, Marriage and Holy Orders), the six necessary points of faith, and the four last things (death, judgement, heaven and hell). While some of the missionaries learned the native tongues to facilitate their teaching, others used interpreters. By royal command, and in alignment with the goal of the colonial system the teaching of Spanish to the Indians was obligatory.

The Catholic Church's work was completely under the power of the Spanish Crown. Though they determined the core of the religious instruction at the missions, the only way a missionary could go to the new world was with royal permission. The equipment and the stipends were under the authority of the King. The crown could even remove missionaries or entire orders at will. The Jesuits, for example, were initially in control of the Missions in the New World. But by the time our story begins the Jesuits had lost favor and their work was given to the Franciscans to continue.

The Mission system under the Spanish Crown was also supported by an independent financial system called "The Pious Fund." Father Juan Maria Salvatierra began soliciting private funds for the Missions while they were still under the leadership of the Jesuits. "The first donation was received from a pious confraternity in Queretaro."[9] Within the next 30 years, 14 missions were started in New Spain, with at least 5 of them endowed by the Marquis de Villapuente alone. In 1764 the Duchess of Gaudia willed her large estate to the fund. In 1766 Josefa Arguellas willed over half a million dollars to the fund. The fund transitioned from the Society of Jesus in 1767 when they were replaced by the Franciscans. Donations, large and small, continued, from private funds of charitable persons whose interest was the conversion and civilization of the Indians in California.

By 1810 this colonization effort resulted in a relatively stabilized life in Los Angeles. There was a symbiotic farming relationship between the Mission and the pueblo including both Spaniards and Native Americans. El Pueblo de la Reina de Los Angeles was a civilian pueblo which played a key role in food production for the region. The pueblo developed wild crops harvested by the indigenous peoples including acorns which were in abundance. The Tongva[10] had worked out a process to remove the bitterness from acorns and transform them into "a mush that provided a nutritious dietary staple."[11] But the relationship between the Spanish and the Tongva was lopsided. As Edward Wicher commented on the role of the Tongva, "In all this activity they were allowed no part in the direction of their work. Everything was planned for them."[12]

The Mission system resulted in the conversion of many groups of Indians. The San Gabriel Mission alone recorded over 25,000 baptisms between 1771 and 1834. But the impact was short lived. When the Spanish missionaries left the region the Native Americans suffered. Robert Speer, wrote: "The Conquerors maintained from the beginning an attitude of superiority over the natives. A system of slavery soon grew up, in justification of which some held that Indians were not rational creatures and had no souls."[13] Matthew Restall and Felipe Fernandez-Armesto wrote: "The Spanish empire, though by no means the most brutal or ill-intentioned in human history, was a terrible affliction for most of the peoples who endured it, and its malign effects are obvious."[14] Edward Wicher, writing in the early 20th century, assesses the long term effects when he says, "It is a pathetic fact that with the passing of the use of the Mission buildings the religious work of the missions has practically disappeared. Today it is impossible to find traces of religious influence exercised by the Padres among the Indians of the state of California."[15]

The collapse of the Mission system as the predominant way of life in what would become Los Angeles had a lot to do with external politics. As Kenneth Latourette put it, "Mexico was disturbed through the repercussions of the Napoleonic wars and eventually broke away from Spanish rule and the missions in California suffered."[16] When Napoleon invaded Spain, the Pious fund was threatened but it continued right down to 1842 when the Mexican government appropriated the remaining money. Under Mexican rule, Los Angeles had to develop a new way of life. This new chapter would be built, not around the Missions, but around ranchos. Pio Pico and Christianity would have to adapt and change.

Boundry Changes in Southern California

On January 8, 1847, Pio Pico purchased the 8,894 Rancho Paso Bartolo. These types of large land purchases began to dominate the area as early as 1821. As the Mission system crumbled, the ranchos began to define the area. The power and wealth in the area was now in the hands of "Dons," the owners of these large ranchos.

The seeds of this new way of life began in the 1780's when Spanish soldier and Governor Pedro Fages assigned huge tracts of land near the San Gabriel mission to three soldiers who had served under his command. The largest grant was made to Manuel Nieto. Rancho Los Nietos covered what would become Long Beach, Downey, Lakewood, Norwalk, Santa Fe Springs, Whittier and a large portion of Orange County. Fages also gave the 75,000-acre Rancho San Pedro to Juan Jose Dominguez. And Jose Maria Verdugo received a 36,000-acre tract which would become known as the Rancho San Rafael: the present-day site of the city of Glendale, in Los Angeles county.[17]

Hugo Reid at Rancho Santa Anita

In this early rancho period, the Mission system still had the backing of the Spanish government. As a result, the Rancheros sought land as far from the Missions as possible. But as power shifted, this quickly changed. When Mexico gained independence from Spain and took over the region, they also began to take land away from the Missions. 1.5 million acres of land was taken from the Mission San Gabriel alone.[18] Many of these land grants were also given to soldiers, who by this time were Mestizos, Hispanicized Indians, freed slaves and "fighting Indians." But they were also given to Mexican citizens. The Rancho Santa Anita, a 13,319-acre rancho, was given to naturalized Scottish immigrant Hugo Reid. His Tongva wife, Victoria, had become a Christian through the San Gabriel Mission, though Hugo Reid would later write a series of newspaper articles criticizing the treatment of the Tongva people by the Franciscans.[19] They built an adobe house on the property that had once been the possession of the Mission.[20]

Life on these ranchos was quite difficult at first. Families would live in small two-bedroom adobe homes, "with thatched roofs, dirt floors, beds made out of leaves, and hides for blankets."[21] Through the years they were able to add ease and then luxury to their lives, while delegating the more difficult work to others, often the Native Americans.

69

In this chapter of life in Los Angeles, the dons formed an elite ruling class who, given their distance from Mexico City, were able to resist government intervention in the area. Jose del Carmen Lugo (1813-c. 1870), for example, was born in Los Angeles when it was still a Spanish pueblo. He and his brothers, Jose Maria and Vicente Lugo, as well as their cousin Diego Sepulveda, held over 250,000 acres of land in the present-day Inland Empire. In 1839 their land charter was approved by the Mexican government. In 1841, the Lugos used the Mexican Secularization Act of 1833 to apply for and receive an additional 35,509 acres known as the Rancho San Bernardino, the former headquarters of farming activity for the Mission San Gabriel. But they had to provide for their own security for the land. Robberies and frequent raids by Indians forced the Lugo family to become strong allies of the Mountain Band of Cahuilla Indians for protection.

A new economy developed around this redistribution of land. Los Angeles became known for its large cattle herds. The mild climate helped the grasses and plants flourish as feed for the cattle. And the cattle were lucrative, not for meat or dairy, but for their hides. Known as "California Banknotes," these cowhides would be taken to San Pedro Bay and traded for cloth, furniture, sugar, whiskey and other products. Trading ships would then transport them to factories in Boston where they would be manufactured into shoes, boots and saddles. These large cattle herds would be found grazing throughout Los Angeles County until the 1860s.

The shift of life from Mission to Rancho also transformed Christianity in the area. Catholicism continued to dominate but in the narrower form of Frontier Catholicism. In place of the integrated strategy of life and ministry among the Spanish and Native Americans in the Catholic Mission System, this form of Catholicism focused on family devotion among Catholic families. This in-house faith would include a home shrine and the cultivation of deep respect for God, the Virgin Mary, the Saints and the clergy.[22] This system also had a strong Catholic organizational structure. In 1859 the resident bishop oversaw a system which included clergy, nuns, outside funding and strong administration. The clergy spoke English as well as the Spanish of the majority population. Community space was structured around a plaza featuring the church. The church bells were regularly rung to call people to congregational prayer. There was also outreach to the remnants of the Native American population in the L.A. area. During this time, they continued to live near the Missions as well as in the poorer parts of the city. There were clergy and lay workers of the Roman Catholic Church working with them. Bringing them into the fold, however, was no longer the priority. Though this form of Catholicism fed the faithful, it was a far cry from the Mission system of days gone by.[23] It would not be able to withstand the chapter that was about to come. For Los Angeles was about to become a part of the United States.

Pio Pico was California's last governor under Mexican rule. In 1848 the U.S. annexed California through the Treaty of Guadalupe Hidalgo, signed at the conclusion of the Mexican-American war. In 1849 the American military Governor, Richard Barnes Mason, appointed Jose del Carmen Lugo as mayor of Los Angeles.[24] Pio Pico and Christianity would have to adapt for a third time.

Pio Pico

By the 1850's, Pio Pico was already one of the richest men in Alta California. He had added the former Mission San Fernando Rey de Espana, Rancho Santa Margarita y Las Flores and several other ranchos to his land holdings. He owned more than 500,000 acres. But life in the area was continuing to change.

U.S rule would have a profound impact on the Ranchos of Los Angeles. The U.S. Congress passed the California land act of 1851, creating a land commission to determine the validity of all land titles from Spanish and Mexican rule. The Eagle Tree, in present day Compton, appears in a legal description in this time. President James Buchanan issued a decree summarizing the northern boundary of the rancho of the Dominguez family in the following way, "Beginning at a sycamore tree, sixty inches in diameter, standing on the East of the road leading to San Pedro..."[25] For many of the rancheros, this new way of doing things would prove onerous. During the rancho period under Mexico it was not unusual to confirm ownership with drawings which specified streams, boulders, and specific trees. But this was not enough under the United States law. The commission required much clearer definitions to justify land ownership. Many of the rancheros could not survive the legal fees and travel expenses required to work through a process which could last 17 years.

This was not the only challenge for the rancheros. The cattle industry was also going through dramatic changes. Texas and Missouri began cattle drives to the San Francisco market. By 1857 demand was overwhelmed and prices plummeted. This drove many of the rancheros into debt. A two-year drought from 1862-1864 caused the rancheros to struggle further. The entire industry went into steep decline. In 1869 there were 70,000 head of cattle in the area. One year later, in 1870, there were only 20,000 head. Los Angeles was no longer the "Queen of the Cow Counties."[26] Instead, private investors came in and bought ranch land for pennies an acre, then broke them into smaller development tracts and sold them for thousands of dollars.

Pio Pico found a way to ride this new wave of change as well. In 1869 he opened what was considered the most lavish hotel in early American Southern California, the three-story, thirty-three room "Casa de Pico." It is in this phase of Pico's life that we hear of Pio Pico and Biddy Mason having occasional dinners together.

Westward expansion under President James K. Polk's Manifest Destiny[27] brought with it a Western democratic liberalism which had been incubating for generations in the rest of the United States. It arrived in force in Los Angeles with the railroad which brought a flood of mid-Westerners to the city. Prior to the railroad, getting to Los Angeles from the Eastern United States was no easy task. Before 1858 the quickest mail route was the Pacific Mail Steamship company which took a letter 25 days to arrive. The overland option took even longer, six months or more. But on September 15, 1857 a six-year contract was signed with the Butterfield Overland Mail Company for semi-weekly service between St. Louis and San Francisco by way of Los Angeles. The idea was to develop a 2,700-mile land route which would take 25 days or less to complete. Many thought it would never happen. But with the support of 100 stages, 1,000 horses, 500 mules and 750 people the stage route began to function, arriving in Los Angeles at the Bella Union Hotel, the leading hotel in the city at the time.[28]

The arrival of the first transcontinental railroad in the 1870s made travel to Los Angeles much easier than any of these options. By the 1880s there were two railroad companies offering transport to the city. A price war developed between the Santa Fe and the Southern Pacific railroads and the price of a ticket dropped significantly. More and more Americans could afford to travel by train to L.A.

The gold rush helped mid-Westerners see California as the land of opportunity. "Just as the rancheros had once viewed mission lands with a covetous eye, American settlers began to see rancho lands as ripe for the taking."[29]

These changes also had a deep impact on Christianity in the city. Los Angeles was predominantly Roman Catholic until the 1880s, though, as mentioned in the previous chapter, it wasn't for lack of trying by Protestants. Frontier Protestantism, which had been quite successful in other parts of the country during Westward expansion just didn't take in the City of Angels.

The first Methodist sermon preached in Los Angeles was by Rev. James W. Brier in June of 1850. His family had travelled overland in an ox cart, surviving the journey through Death Valley. Other members of the "Jayhawkers," as they were known, died from cold and lack of food on the way. They had failed to get to the Sierra Nevada before the snowfall and had to take the more perilous route. Upon arrival, the Methodist minister advertised a service of worship in a local home. Out of the 274 citizens of Los Angeles at the time, the only people in attendance were the Nichols family, who were the hosts, and Brier's wife and three children. When Brier held the second service in the courthouse, not even the Nichols' family attended. In 1852 John G. Nichols would become the Mayor of Los Angeles. Three months after their first two worship services, the Brier family left for Northern California.[30]

On the 18th of March 1855, Rev. James Woods organized a Presbyterian church in Los Angeles with 12 members; the first body to formally constitute themselves as a Protestant congregation in the city. By September of that year Rev. Woods had to move out of the city because of poor health. In 1856 Thomas K. Davis replaced him. He was followed soon after by Rev. William Boardman. In 1859 the congregation was dispersed and in 1863 the church was sold at the Sheriff's auction for non-payment of taxes. The *Los Angeles Star*, writing about the sale, said, "What heathens we must be, sure enough, when we find the church offered for sale by the sheriff."[31]

But with the completion of the railroad all of this would change. Protestant pastors who had previously struggled to start churches finally had the numbers to build their congregations as those who were already converted arrived from other parts of the country. This chapter in the history of Christianity in Los Angeles, probably the best attested of any period in the city, is covered in detail in the next chapter. For now, we will look at broad aspects of the way of life which developed in this period and continue to have an impact on the city today.

Early Los Angeles, under U.S. governance, continued the tradition begun by the ranchers and businessmen during the Rancho period who themselves took the responsibility of caring for the poor who were referred to them, particularly after natural disasters. As one commentator notes, "Probably the most remarkable of the private philanthropists was Biddy Mason."[32] As this third period continued, there was an attempt to build voluntary societies which would integrate newcomers into the wider society.

The idea of society as a "melting pot" had been in use since at least 1780. American farmer J. Hector St. Jon de Crevecouer asked the question:

> What then is the American, this new man?" Then he answered by writing that the American is one who "leaving behind him all his ancient prejudices and manners, receives new ones from the new mode of life he has embraced, the government he obeys, and the new rank he holds. He becomes an American by being received in the broad lap of our great Alma Mater. Here individuals of all nations are

melted into a new race of men, whose labors and posterity will one day cause great changes in the world.[33]

A magazine article in 1876 used the metaphor explicitly:

The fusing process goes on as in a blast-furnace; one generation, a single year even—transforms the English, the German, the Irish emigrant into an American. Uniform institutions, ideas, language, the influence of the majority, bring us soon to a similar complexion; the individuality of the immigrant, almost even his traits of race and religion, fuse down in the democratic alembic like chips of brass thrown into the melting pot.[34]

There was great hope in this metaphor. America was a place where minorities, though not yet members of the middle and upper class of the country, could nevertheless aspire to move beyond their own social and economic heritage and share in the American dream. In 1931 James Truslow Adams wrote that "life should be better, richer and fuller for everyone, with opportunity for each according to his ability or achievement."[35]

Volunteer societies were the "feet on the ground" of such an idea. In 1907 Dana W. Bartlett observed, "The rising power of the common man is being recognized first by settlement and Civic Association rather than by Church and Cathedral."[36] Much of this had begun decades earlier in the city. In 1877, 34 years before women gained the right to vote in the United States, 63 women formed the Protestant Benevolent Society. It self-described as "a non-denominational organization to raise money for charitable purposes."[37] The funds were largely gained from annual fees paid by its members. In the 1880s philanthropic organizations like this began to grow rapidly in the city. "In 1883 the Women's Christian Temperance Union advocated women's rights and, with other women's clubs, challenged employers by advocating child labor laws and minimum wages for women."[38] In that same year the first Protestant orphanage opened in Los Angeles, the Los Angeles Orphans Home Society sponsored by the Los

Angeles Women's Club. In 1892 the Midnight Mission and the Union Rescue Mission for the homeless and destitute began. Other voluntary organizations included the Sojourner Truth Home for young Negro women, the Methodist Mission in Los Angeles supported by ten denominations and focused on Chinese girls, the Jane Couch Memorial Home for homeless Japanese girls, and the Forsythe Memorial School for the care of Mexican girls, established by the Women's Missionary Society of the Presbytery Church. The YWCA was established in this time as well as a variety of "institutions for children, settlement houses like Brownson House that focused on the Americanization of Immigrants; Ransome House originally founded by the Social Purity League, as a refuge for young women and children; various hospitals, and art and cultural facilities."[39] Many of these organizations no longer exist. But this form of voluntary society continues to have an impact on the city. Some, like the Union Rescue Mission, continue to play an important role in the city today, more than 100 years after its formation. But there is remains a serious question about how deep the adaptation really went.

Letitia Burns O'Conner wrote:

> Los Angeles is a frontier town. Whether out of necessity or a desire for adventure, people come here--as they have from the city's very beginning--to start anew. They bring with them the comfort of their own ways as much as a desire to shed the baggage of the past. As a result, even mainstream religions have been forced to come to terms with the essential uniqueness of the city's faithful.[40]

Though true, to some extent, our survey points in a different direction. The Missions held to a paternalism which enforced a Spanish pattern of life rather than allowing Native Americans to turn their own ancient culture toward Christ. Frontier Catholicism simply reinforced a form a Catholicism developed elsewhere. The Protestant churches tended to meet according to their sociocultural demographic, reinforcing rather than challenging the racial and social barriers mid-Western Christians brought with them to Los Angeles. Though these societies are admirable in trying to help others adapt to this new way of life, one has to note their limited effect as part of the "melting pot" idea in U.S. history. The question remains as to whether Christianity has ever really adapted to the peculiar qualities of Los Angeles. The different forms of Christianity found in L.A. were all developed outside of the city and only later brought into the City of Angels. Christianity took hold, it seems, not because it successfully adapted to Los Angeles, but because some portion of L.A. adapted to its forms.

Dr. Andrew Walls, in correspondence with Ghanaian theologian Dr. Kwame Bediako, wrote:

> Conversion is not about adopting someone else's pattern of life and thought, however ancient and however excellent, that is not conversion but proselytization...conversion involves the turning towards Christ of everything that is there already, so that Christ comes into places, thoughts, relationships, and world-views in which he has never lived before.[41]

Has conversion, as Walls uses the term, ever really occurred in Los Angeles or would it be more accurate to say that Christianity has proselytized three different chapters of life in the city?

The challenge of a Christianity that truly develops out of the soil of Los Angeles is still before us. Conversion in the City of Angels is complicated. L.A. has always been a city with challenges that Christianity hasn't had to deal with in other parts of the country. Michael Eng, in his book *Frontier Faiths*, points out that Los Angeles had a great ethnic and racial diversity earlier than other frontier towns. The first Chinese Temple, for example, was established in Los Angeles in 1875 to serve an estimated 170 Chinese immigrants, many of whom had already lived in the city for 25 years as "house servants" for the Anglo-American settlers. Chinese religion, at this time, was a blend of Buddhist, Confucian and Taoist teachings. The Protestants in the city were largely unfamiliar even with Spanish, much less Chinese language or culture. Frontier Protestantism simply wasn't prepared for ministry to such a diverse community.

Perhaps this is where the opportunity lies for Christianity in Los Angeles. Christianity has proven its ability to make its home in cultures around the world, including China. Christianity in Los Angeles, as we saw in the previous chapter, has already transcended barriers of racial, ethnic and gender diversity in people like Biddy Mason. It has also worked through the existing structures as we saw in the miracle mile. Perhaps the time is ripe in the 21st century for Christianity to help Los Angeles embrace its multi-ethnicity. We will focus on this possibility in chapter 8.

Another perennial struggle in L.A. where Christianity can contribute is what we have called "the Los Angeles turn." The theme continues to run strongly through this chapter's narrative. In the shift from the Missions to the ranchos, the dreams of the Spanish and the missionaries went unfulfilled as the Missions fell into ruin and the ranchos and dons rose to take their place. In the transition from ranchos to liberal Western democracy under the United States, the dons suffered the same fate. Lugo's life, for example, took a Los Angeles turn. In 1854 Lugo was in desperate need of money. He signed a note at five percent interest per month, compounded monthly, and mortgaged the rest of his property including his home in L.A. His financial troubles continued and he lost his house and his land to cover the original note. He died in poverty in 1870. Even Pio Pico, who managed to transition through all three chapters of Los Angeles, was finally hit by the L.A. turn. Like Lugo, he died in near poverty. Gambling losses, losses to loan sharks, bad business practices, and the 1883 floods forced him to liquidate his real estate holdings. He spent his final years in the home of his daughter. He died in Los Angeles in 1894 at 93 years of age. We will look more at Christianity and the L.A. turn in chapter 7.

Christianity, like Pico, has left a mark on the city. Three times Christianity has adapted to Los Angeles: to colonization under Spanish rule, to the ranchos under Mexico, and to the Westward expansion of liberal democratic governance of the United States. Like the Eagle Tree, Christianity continues in L.A. But as we shall see in the next chapter, Christianity in the City of Angels has begun a new chapter; a chapter in which many church buildings have been repurposed as homes, dance clubs and boutique hotels.[42] The faith needs to adapt again. And this maybe the most challenging adaptation yet.

Chapter 5
Stuck in La La Land

. . . it is past its prime already. It has lost the exuberant certainty that made it seem unarguably the City of the Future, the City That Knew How. None of us know now. The machine has lost its promise of emancipation, and if L.A. then seemed a talisman of fulfillment, now it is tinged with disillusion. Those terrific roads, those thousands of cars, the sheen of jets screaming out of the airport, the magnificent efficiency of it all, the image building, the self-projection, the glamor, the fame--they were all false promises after all, and few of us see them now as the symptoms of redemption. -Jan Morris[1]

Protestant Christianity thrived in the first half of the 20th century. By the beginning of the 21st these churches were in decline. Many have now joined the Mission ruins and the old "plaza church" of frontier Catholicism as signs of the perennial challenge before so much of life in L.A.; adapting to the "next thing" in the City of Angels.

Mission Santa Fe

In the early 20th century Los Angeles was the land of opportunity. The infrastructure for success was laid down. In 1904 vast tracts of the San Fernando Valley were purchased and developed by a syndicate which included then editor of the *Los Angeles Times*, Harry Chandler.[2] At the time of purchase the land was considered worthless. But the syndicate had advance notice of a renewed plan to irrigate the valley with water from the nearby Owens River Valley. This irrigation allowed vast development, not only of their purchase, but of the entire region. Chandler and his business partners would make a profit of more than $100,000,000 on the project.

William Mulholland, the city's chief water engineer once said, "whoever brings the water will bring the people."[3] It took 5,000 workers five years to complete the irrigation job on time and under budget; "215 miles of road, 280 miles of pipeline, 142 tunnels, more than 1 million barrels of cement and 6 million pounds of dynamite."[4] This water system allowed Los Angeles to spread out with networks of roads, freeways and cars. It also formed the basis for the movie *Chinatown* which did much to spread the idea that Los Angeles was a city on a desert. As Mayor Bagby in the movie says, "Remember—we live next door to the ocean but we also live on the edge of the desert. Los Angeles is a desert community. Beneath this building, beneath every street there's a desert. Without water the dust will rise up and cover us as though we'd never existed!"

The motion picture industry moved to Los Angeles in this period. In 1923 Harry Chandler built the Hollywood sign to advertise another development; this time a segregated housing subdivision in the hills above Hollywood. In the early 1920's Walter Elias Disney moved from his hometown of Chicago to Los Angeles, developing the character Mickey Mouse in 1928 and producing *Snow White and the Seven Dwarves*, *Pinnochio* and *Fantasia* in the next 13 years. In 1955 he opened Disneyland with the corporate motto, "where dreams come true."

Beyond real estate and movies, oil was a major economic engine for the economy of L.A. in this time. It may be difficult to imagine today, but Los Angeles was once covered in oil derricks. Three years after the first Academy Awards were held in the Blossom Room of the Roosevelt Hotel in 1928, a *Los Angeles Times* article read:

> Today oil derricks stand like trees in a forest... Steam pile drivers roar on many a vacant lot... One hundred and eighty permits to drill for oil have been given and twenty-five more are in procedure... If this fever continues, as it gives every indication of doing, one reasonably may expect to see virtually the entire water-front line of private properties from Washington street to Sixty-sixth avenue of Playa del Rey dotted with a line of oil derricks.[5]

Edward Doheny, who drilled the first oil well in Los Angeles, became incredibly wealthy. His philanthropy paid for many enduring institutions in Los Angeles, including the USC Memorial Library. The Carrie Estelle Doheny Foundation, named after Doheny's wife, still contributes around $8 million a year to non-profits working to advance education, health, medicine, religion and vulnerable populations almost exclusively in Los Angeles.

Oil Derricks in early Los Angeles

Architecture also thrived. Cutting edge architects were hired to build highly creative structures in the city. In 1924, Frank Lloyd Wright's 6,000 square foot Mayan themed Ennis House was built in Los Feliz. Los Angeles was, as Morris put it, "the City that Knew How."

After World War II the city and its infrastructure grew exponentially. The economy included manufacturing, aerospace, and automobile products. The emerging apparel industry and to a lesser extent the continuation of the oil industry and agriculture in Los Angeles propelled a postwar economic explosion. Los Angeles also began to go global. In 1959 Ruth Handler introduced the Barbie doll to an international audience. The emergence of surfing culture and the Beach Boys did much to promote the L.A. dream not only in California and the United States but beyond. The city embodied the idea that the individual is free to pursue their own conception of the good life.

The most readily available stories of Protestant Christianity in Los Angeles come from this period of expansion. In 1870 there were only five fully organized Protestant churches in Los Angeles. By 1890 there were 44 church organizations from 12 different denominations. As the 20th century began, the difficulties and challenges of the first Protestant pastors were giving way to familiar success stories of well-known ministers like Aimee Semple McPherson, Billy Graham, and the early radio preachers.

In 1895, near Bologne, Italy, Guglielmo Marconi sent his first wireless message on his family estate. At first, this new technology was used mainly for shipping communications. By 1912 the practical uses of radio in modern society still hadn't become clear. However, as new commercial uses for radio were being developed, Christians began to experiment with it as a new means for ministry.

Guglielmo Marconi

The first commercial radio station went on air in Pittsburgh in 1920. Just one year later, Christians in Los Angeles began to experiment with the wireless. In 1908 Lyman Steward, president of Union Oil, and Presbyterian ministers Thomas C. Horton and Augustus Prichard, founded the Bible Institute of Los Angeles (Biola) to train students in Bible and Christian mission. In 1921 R. E. Carrier, an engineer at Biola, convinced Dean Reuben Torrey and founder Thomas Horton to construct a radio station.[6] In 1922 it became the first radio station devoted specifically to religious broadcasting. There were plenty of misgivings about mingling Christianity and this new technology. One year after the opening of the station, Thomas Horton himself wrote an article entitled, "Restless Over Radio." In that article he listed a number of objections to this ministry:

1. It would give one preacher too much prominence.
2. It is costly and draws money away from other Christian enterprises.
3. It creates a "stay-at-home" habit.
4. It deprives the listener of that personal contact with the preacher himself.
5. Can't follow up decisions for Christ as effectively.
6. When radio is used for all kinds of commercial purposes and amusements it is questionable whether the gospel should use it as well.
7. Should the gospel be preached over the air waves when Satan is the prince of the power of the air?[7]

Perhaps somewhat surprisingly, at the end of the article, Horton gives a cautious seal of approval.

Biola

Other radio ministries developed in Los Angeles in future years, including *Haven of Rest* with Paul Myers in 1934 and *The Old Fashioned Revival Hour* with Biola graduate Dr. Charles Fuller in 1937. Radio vastly expanded the reach of these preachers. When asked how many people he had preached to since going on radio, Dr. Charles Fuller replied, "I don't know about the figure, whether it's right or not, but the radio officials tell me that my audience runs twenty million a Sunday...the Lord will tell me when I get to glory."[8]

Of course, this was not the first time "means" were used in Los Angeles to spread the news of God's love in Christ. We saw, in chapter three, how tents had been used in Los Angeles in the early 1900's. Tents had been a part of Christianity in the United States since at least the 1800's when tent revivals or camp meetings brought religion to frontier areas in states like Kentucky and Ohio that lacked established churches. By the 1920's tent meetings were effectively used to "stir up the faithful by creating an almost circus-like atmosphere" and "to attract new congregants who would be moved by the message to join a local church."[9]

Billy Graham brought his tent revival ministry to Los Angeles in 1949. "I'm convinced...that if a revival could break out in the city of Los Angeles," he wrote to Mr. Claude Jenkins, the secretary of the local committee who sought to bring him to L.A., "it would have repercussions around the world."[10]

At first it appeared that Graham's Los Angeles crusade would be a non-event. The local committee set up press conferences with reporters, but unlike J.L. Griffin many decades earlier, they couldn't even get an article in the paper. Just before the campaign started, however, a meeting was held which would change everything.

Miss Henrietta Mears invited Graham to her home in Beverly Hills to speak to a group of Christians from Hollywood.[11] She was the Director of Christian Education at First Presbytery Church, Hollywood. Under her leadership the Sunday school attendance at the church grew from 400 to 6,500. Her ministry was profoundly influential in the ministries of Bill Bright (Campus Crusade for Christ), Jim Rayburn (Young Life), and Louis Evans Jr. (founding pastor of Bel Air Presbyterian Church and later pastor of National Presbyterian Church in Washington, D.C.). She founded the Gospel Light publishing company, the Forest Home Christian Conference Center, and Gospel Literature International.[12] Billy Graham accepted her invitation.

At this meeting Graham met the man who gave the tent meetings all the publicity they needed. Stuart Hamblen, the son of a Methodist minister in Texas, was a composer and an actor. He was in a number of movies with cowboy stars including Gene Autry, Roy Rogers, and John Wayne. In 1931 he continued to develop his career by hosting the popular radio program, *Family Album*, in California. In 1934 he became the first artist signed by the American subsidiary of Decca Records. Like many before him in Los Angeles, Hamblen's dream was becoming reality.

But Hamblen was not coping well with the pressures of his high-profile career. His drinking landed him in jail for numerous offenses. Hamblen began calling himself the "original juvenile delinquent."[13] But he was so popular on the radio that his sponsors stuck with him and would regularly bail him out of jail. Then he began gambling. His life and his career began suffering.

Hamblen met Graham at the gathering. But it wasn't until 1949, after attending Graham's tent crusade multiple times, that he committed his life to Christ. It was this conversion, not his previous "delinquency," which got him fired from his radio show. As a Christian and recovering alcoholic he refused to do beer commercials and was let go. After giving up gambling and horse racing as well, Hamblen began a Christian radio show, *The Cowboy Church of the Air*, which continued until 1952.

In 1963, Billy Graham said Hamblen's conversion was the turning point in the L.A. tent crusades. It was Hamblen's conversion which caught the attention of publishing magnate William Randolph Hearst. Hearst made sure his newspapers gave full coverage to Graham's evangelistic campaign. As a result, Graham gained the attention, not only of Los Angeles, but of the entire nation.

Aimee Semple McPherson is another well-known minister from this time period who worked outside of traditional church ministry. "Sister Aimee," as she was known, began her ministry outside of Los Angeles, in cities like Chicago and Baltimore. She believed that she could gather her followers from these cities and more in one congregation in Los Angeles. Her dream was fulfilled. She built the $1.5 million Angelus Temple in the early 1920's where she continued her trailblazing ministry. Not only was she a female preacher, but she was the first woman to preach on the radio. Not only did she use methods from stage acts and movies in her services but she also is credited with bringing popular music into the church, including jazz. Her congregation transcended social barriers at that time by gathering both black and white members in the same congregation, as well as Mexican immigrants and people of many other nationalities.

Aimee Semple McPherson

These were the glory days of Los Angeles. They were also the high point of Modern American Protestantism in the city. But just below the surface simmered consistent problems which were about to boil. Economic divisions and the attitudes that reinforced them surfaced as early as 1907. In a sociological study of Los Angeles from that time, entitled, "A Better City" the Rev. Dana Bartlett writes, "The City of Angels is as yet far away from the ideal city. The dollar still rules. Material things are still more sought for than the spiritual. Low political ideals still hold sway."[14]

A few decades later Charles Reznikoff, a poet who lived in Los Angeles from 1937-1940, wrote:

> These gentlemen are great; they are paid
> a dollar a minute. They will not answer
> if you say, Good morning;
> will neither smile nor nod--
> if you are paid only a dollar or two
> an hour (study
> when to be silent, when to smile.)
> The employer who greets my employer loudly
> and smiles broadly, reaching for his hand and back,
> scowls and glares at my greeting. Now I understand
> why he managed to give me only his fingers
> when we were introduced. Why do you go to such trouble
> to teach me that you are great?
> I never doubted it until now.[15]

The pluralism of the city was not integrated; instead the "problem" of ethnicity was contained in "silos" in different sections of the city. In the 1940s 95% of housing in Los Angeles was off limits to African-Americans and Asians. They were only allowed to live in East or South Los Angeles, including an area called Watts. The courts ruled these "racial restrictive covenants" illegal in 1948. But they continued to be practiced, if not supported legally afterwards. The "melting pot," for these populations, did not apply.

The "Los Angeles turn" also contributed to the underlying problems of the City of Dreams. Aimee Semple McPherson, for example, disappeared for a period of time under suspicious circumstances. For 5 weeks in 1926, after a visit to Venice Beach, no one knew where she was. Then she reappeared in Mexico claiming she had escaped from kidnappers who had held her for ransom. After her reappearance she continued her ministry though the disappearance remained a bit of a mystery. In 1944, shortly after preaching a sermon, she was found dead in her hotel room. At 54 years of age she was the victim of an accidental overdose of prescription barbiturates.

In the summer of 1965 all of these issues boiled over. Watts exploded into a racial battlefield after an African-American driver was arrested on suspected DUI. A minor argument grew into a fight. Angelenos in the neighborhood responded to allegations of police brutality with six days of looting and arson. It was one of the most violent and costly riots in U.S. history. It was only the first sign that Los Angeles was stuck.

In 1968 Robert F. Kennedy was assassinated at the Ambassador Hotel by Sirhan Sirhan. Some scholars call this the first major violence in the country derived from the Arab-Israeli conflict. Sirhan, born into an Arab Palestinian family in Jerusalem, said he did it for his country. He felt betrayed by Kennedy's support for the Six-Day War of June 1967.[16]

In 1969 Charles Manson and his followers committed their notorious murders in the Topanga, Beverly Hills, and Silver Lake neighborhoods of L.A. The Manson family believed that the killings would stir up tensions between whites and blacks and thus precipitate the "Helter Skelter apocalyptic race war."

By 1980 the population of the city grew to over 3,000,000, surpassing Chicago as the second largest city in the nation. Part of this growth was due to large scale immigration. Cultural enclaves deepened in Los Angeles. And, at least among low-skilled workers, tension grew around competition for a limited number of jobs. Ann Cudd, in her book, *Analyzing Oppression*, points out that those who have little mobility by virtue of their membership in a particular social group cannot experience the hope or possibility of the melting pot. That vision is only for those who are already included.[17] This dream of the melting pot no longer inspired the city. It gave way to other narratives of inclusion in Los Angeles.

The idea of the "salad bowl" began to develop in the 1960s. This view argued that cultures come together in the United States like the ingredients of a salad. Unlike the "melting pot" idea, they do not form together into a single homogeneous culture. This narrative was given a voice in the 1991 film entitled, *Grand Canyon*. Los Angeles was the "stage" for this film. The movie featured characters from different races and classes in the city. Each character experienced the city uniquely, as a result of their race and class. The movie traces their experiences of each other's Los Angeles. Eventually, all of the characters take a road trip to the Grand Canyon to celebrate a new philosophy that is bigger than their separate lives. This same philosophy is told by Alan Wolf as if it were a children's story.

> Once upon a time, it is said, such societies were ruled by privileged elites. Governing circles were restricted to those of the correct gender, breeding, education, and social exclusiveness. All this changes as a result of those multiple forces identified by the term democracy. First the middle classes, then working men, then women, and then racial minorities will win, not only economic rights, but also political and social rights.[18]

This story would spawn new movements in search of justice and human rights.

Two other closely related and even overlapping approaches to plurality have also become prominent, not only in the United States, but in Europe as well: multiculturalism and identity politics. Multiculturalism is most commonly understood as a society in which various ethnic groups collaborate with one another without having to sacrifice their particular identities. The term "identity politics" rose to prominence in the 1970s. This approach attempts to correct the flaws of the "melting pot" by claiming that individuals belonging to certain groups by virtue of their identity are more vulnerable to oppression. It encourages these people to express their experience of oppression by a process of consciousness-raising.

These new dreams, however, were overshadowed by harsh reality as riots rocked Los Angeles again in 1992. The popular history of these riots focus on the white police officers beating of Rodney King, an African-American. But Brenda Stevenson, a UCLA historian, argues that this was only the flashpoint for the riots. A previous event, she says, had already set the scene. On March 16, 1991, 15-year old Latasha Harlins was in a store run by Soon Ja Du, a middle-aged Korean woman. The shop keeper was convinced that Harlins was trying to steal a bottle of juice and confronted her. After a fight, Harlins was shot in the back of the head and killed. Police found $2.00 in her hand, the price of the juice. Soon Ja Du was convicted of felony manslaughter. But she served no jail time.[19] Less than a year later, on April 29, 1992, Los Angeles was torn apart by looting and arson. The National Guard was deployed and martial-law was established. L.A. became an urban war zone for more than three days. Fifty-five people died, more than 2,300 were injured and 1,100 buildings were damaged at a cost of over $1 billon.

Angelenos continued to struggle in other ways in the 1990's. In 1994 a 6.7 magnitude earthquake in Northridge caused $20 billion in property damage. The rise of gang culture in the city took its toll with 807 gang-related deaths in 1995. Firing guns and police helicopters became common in many communities in Los Angeles. By 2001 Los Angeles was the obvious location for the movie *Training Day*. This police drama featured Denzel Washington as a veteran officer escorting a rookie on his first day with LAPD's tough inner-city narcotics unit. The film challenges the viewer to decide what is heroic and what is over-the-line when it comes to fighting urban crime.

Los Angeles changed dramatically as it moved through this tumultuous time. Edward Soja writes, in *My Los Angeles*, that the Rodney King riots: "announced to the world that the post-war economic boom in the United States and elsewhere was not going to continue with business as usual, for too many benefitted too little from the boom." He notes three dramatic shifts in the character of the city during this time. Each was influenced by the new dreams of multiculturalism and identity politics. L.A. went from pro-business and anti-labor to becoming the leading center for national labor movements, especially with regards to gender equality, gay rights, and above all, organization of immigrants. Second, the city moved from automobile-based urbanism to neighborhood identities, place-based politics, and the activities of community-based organizations. Finally, in the years since the Watts riots, L.A. shifted from being the least dense and most sprawling city to the leading example of regional urbanization. He concludes by saying, "Beyond all doubt, Los Angeles is no longer what it used to be."[20]

At this writing, Los Angeles, shifts and all, still feels like the "Knew How City." When an Angelino drives down Hollywood Boulevard it is embarrassing. Large numbers of tourists explore the city block which includes Grauman's Chinese Theater and the footprints and signatures of Humphrey Bogart, Lauren Bacall and many others from the golden years. But all around the theater are seedy stores filled with entertainment industry tchotchkes. On the sidewalks are starving artists rather poorly dressed as the latest action figures hoping to be paid to pose with visitors. In the evenings metal shutters are pulled down over the store fronts. Many of them are decorated with pictures of movies stars and directors of the 1940s. But, like the area, the pictures are time-worn. Some are painted over by graffiti. Is this the best the city can do to represent an industry that has such a legendary past? Maybe the legendary past of Hollywood existed only for some. It certainly doesn't exist today, even as a facade.

Protestant Christianity in Los Angeles has a similar "knew how" feel. Presbyterian minister Ken Baker shared a telling story of Protestant Churches in the aftermath of the 1992 riots. There was a bump in attendance after the riots in many congregations. In conversation with the pastors of some of these congregations, Baker heard them share excitedly about 30 or 40 new members. They were saying, "All of my hard work is finally bearing fruit." Not long afterwards, however, the numbers went back down to pre-riot levels. Baker watched as these pastors became even more discouraged than before. Now, in the 21st century, many churches find themselves in the same predicament as Immanuel Presbyterian. Their past is so beautifully expressed in their church campuses. But in the present, they are struggling to survive.[21] The future of the churches of L.A. is far from certain. The wider organizational structures developed to support the growth of these congregations; seminaries, Presbyteries, Diocese' and the like, are in a struggle for survival as well. The forms of Christianity which developed during the rise of the "Know How" period are stuck in La La Land.

Rev. Ken Baker is the Chief Executive of the Presbytery of San Fernando, one of seven Presbyteries in Los Angeles County. A Presbytery, as Ken describes it, is "an organic union, an organization of interlocking non-profit organizations which have joint and several liability for one another." "This structure," he continues, "made great sense in an earlier era because you had people who could resource and supervise this organization of legally interrelated organizations. Corporate CEOs, successful entrepreneurs, people with full time jobs with good benefits...who could be available at night for meetings, on weekends for church ministries and activities." But the context has radically changed.

The number of congregations in the Presbyterian Church (USA), for example, has been in steady decline since 1965. In that year there were 4.25 million members of the PC(USA) across the country. In 2016 they numbered less than 1.5 million. According to Baker, these congregations and church structures are going through a grieving process. The congregations in L.A. are become increasingly aware of the fact that the period of Protestant expansion in Los Angeles isn't coming back. At first this realization is seen as negative and the churches respond defensively. But over time, defensiveness gives way to acceptance that this is just the way it is. "It doesn't feel good," says Baker, "as it did when things were on an upswing."

But Rev. Baker is optimistic about the future. The Presbytery of San Fernando, like most other Presbyteries, is experiencing decline. But they have also initiated some fresh experiments beyond the institutional structures developed in this period. Baker sees the Presbytery of San Fernando as "a 20th century organization of churches transforming into a 21st century network of ministries." It remains an open question whether these mainline churches and structures can succeed in this transition.

The Dolby Theater was originally named the Kodak Theater. The Eastman Kodak Company signed a $75 million naming-deal with the newly built theater on Hollywood Boulevard in 2001. But Kodak had already peaked in the late 1980s. Their business climate changed dramatically. They didn't. The company that played such a leading role in popularizing film was unable to adapt to the new digital film market. They were stuck. In 2012 Kodak, founded in 1888, filed for Chapter 11 bankruptcy protection. They also lost the naming-rights to the theater. The Kodak Theater was rechristened The Dolby Theater, after the company, started in 1965, that specialized in audio encoding and compression.

The institutional forms, which supported Protestant Christianity in the early 20th century of Los Angeles, are going through the same challenge as Kodak.[22] Will they become "unstuck" and adapt to the changing context? Or will their most majestic buildings become, like the Spanish Missions, museums to a bygone era? Both Los Angeles and Christianity in Los Angeles will have to change and adapt if they are going to thrive in this next generation.

In the remaining chapters of this book, we will consider four ways that Christianity and Los Angeles can work together to adapt to the changes that are already upon them. Using the concept of genealogy as well as the biblical stories of Jonah, Melchizedek and the "future city" of Revelation we will explore ways in which Christianity might work symbiotically with the City of Angels to overcome a number of perennial problems. If L.A. can find a new way to share a common identity that transcends ideological polarization, if they can learn to embrace a more inclusive narrative of the city, and if Los Angeles can find new meaning in the L.A. turn, then the City of Angels can again become the "Know How" city.

Lovejoy

Chapter 6

The Genealogy of El Pueblo de Nuestra Señora la

Reina de los Angeles sobre el Rio de Porciuncula

We are caught in an inescapable mutuality. Whatever effects one directly,

affects all indirectly. All life is interrelated.

Martin Luther King Jr.[1]

This is how the birth of Los Angeles came about: Father Junipero Serra received permission from Carlos Francisco de Croix, the viceroy of New Spain, to establish a new Mission in California near the Rio Nombre de Jesus de los Temblores, not far from the Indian village of Yang Na. Father Angel de Somera and Father Pedro Benito Cambon, along with 14 soldiers and 4 muleteers, left San Diego on August 6, 1770 for the new site of the San Gabriel Mission. In time settlers from this Mission would venture forth to found El Pueblo de la Reyna Los Angeles and the modern city of Los Angeles would be born. For some this is a reason to celebrate. For others it is a reason to mourn.

Fast forward 200 years, to the late 1980's, and we find Pope John Paul II planning a trip to Los Angeles, now a city of more than 2.9 million people. The Pope was coming to beatify Father Serra, already considered a Saint in Catholic spiritual biography.[2] This was a natural next step for this life which should be revered and celebrated. Or so the Catholic Church thought. Instead, a controversy erupted between sharply conflicting views of Serra, of the Missions and ultimately of the origins of Los Angeles. One letter to the editor entitled "The Charges Against Father Junipero Serra,"[3] indicted him for forced castration of Indian males for the benefit of Spanish migration, whippings and physical abuse of the Native Americans, and spreading disease through contaminated blankets while withholding medications. All of this, the article said, was mission policy under Junipero Serra.

William H. Hannon, a Roman Catholic philanthropist and real estate developer, spoke at a dedication of a statue of Father Serra at the Mission San Fernando Rey in 1998. Given all of the friction surrounding Jumipero Serra and the Missions, he found difficulty in talking about the subject of the sculpture in a way that everyone could agree upon. "The man," he said, "was the first real estate developer in Los Angeles if you think about it."4

Junipero Serra

Serra the saint or Serra the oppressor: Two radically different interpretations of the founding of the city. These two voices reflect a deeper polarization in Western culture. The "social temperature" surrounding this issue has given this author pause in even raising the subject. But this inability to celebrate a common sense of identity is part of what keeps L.A. from moving forward. If Los Angeles is going to do more than reflect the political dead ends of U.S. political options, it must find a united voice which transcends these social barriers. The city must find a way to write a shared narrative of the past, present, and future. Christianity can help with this challenge.

Many stereotypes of Christianity attempt to lock the faith into one political position or another. It is important to remember, however, that Christianity has been influential across the continuum from liberalism and conservatism. In the National Statuary Hall in Washington, D.C., every state is represented by two sculptures. Up until 2006 California was represented by Junipero Serra and Thomas Starr King.[5]

King is credited with saving California for the Union side of the American Civil War.[6] He also played a critical role in liberalism. "We can say with confidence that Starr King laid a foundation for liberal Christianity in the California tradition."[7]

On the other end of the spectrum, we return to Lyman Stewart, whom we have already met in a previous chapter. Stewart was a very successful businessman, having made a number of successful oil investments in Los Angeles through Union Oil Company. He was a member of Immanuel Presbyterian Church.[8] He also played a key role in the development of Christian fundamentalism.

In 1909 he provided funds for a book, written by 64 different authors representing most major Christian denominations, to be a "new statement of the fundamentals of Christianity."[9] In 1910, Stewart began to distance himself from denominational agencies, complaining of increasing doctrinal laxity in the denomination's schools and seminaries and, according to E.R. Sandeen, acting on "his conviction that ministers and missionaries were no longer receiving an adequate grounding in the Bible."[10] From 1910-1915 another eleven volumes were published; three million copies in all. They were distributed, free of charge, to Christians in various positions of leadership. They became a symbolic point of reference for identifying the "fundamentalist" movement.[11]

Christianity is a movement which transcends ideological constructs of any age. It is not unusual for influential parts of the church to affiliate themselves with opposing sides of the issues as they have in our day. Very often, however, the adaptability of Christian gospel causes Christians committed to one side or the other to join in the ideological polarization by demonizing the Christians with whom they do not agree.

But when viewed from a global, rather than a national perspective, it becomes clear that Christianity is an ancient and world-wide movement which does not fit neatly into human constructs. It has an ability to make itself at home in any culture, while at the same time challenging any context in which it makes its home.

> Along with the indigenizing principle which makes his faith a place to feel at home, the Christian inherits the pilgrim principle, which whispers to him that he has no abiding city and warns him that to be faithful to Christ will put him out of step with his society.[12]

It is essential to understand that Christianity has a different starting point than any human construct. It does not look for fulfillment in any human movement. It's starting point and method is God's revelation. It also looks for a different ending point. It seeks a social structure that transcends every other social construct. It seeks the Kingdom of God.

This enables Christians to make deeply radical statements such as the following by one of the greatest theologians of the 20th century, Dr. Karl Barth.

> As yet we see but the image of this world and its domination. Mighty it is, and lifted up and very magnificent, terrible to behold, an image of gold and silver, of iron and clay and brass. But in the hidden life of Jesus we see also the stone fashioned and detached, which smites the image on its feet and, without any aid from human hands, breaks it into pieces. The whole image is crushed, and the wind carries it away like the chaff of the summer threshing floors.[13]

Radical, but in a very Christian way.

It is this "genius" of Christianity which earned condemnation in its early contact with the Roman Empire. Roman converts did not worship the Roman gods, including the "divine emperor." Therefore, according to some Romans, they were atheists. It is this genius which gives Christianity in Los Angeles the potential to help the city become "unstuck." This chapter is written in the hopes of helping Christianity in Los Angeles to re-engage this genius. To do so we need a new way to envision Los Angeles. We can begin by engaging the concept of "genealogy."

Genealogy is a popular way to understand our lives. Tracing our lineage can focus our sense of identity, meaning and purpose as we move forward. The 20th century French philosopher, Michel Foucalt turned to genealogy to understand and evaluate, not a particular individual, but a particular culture. He found that genealogy could help to discredit ideas from the past which had become cultural assumptions in the present. In his hands genealogy was a mild acid which dissolved unjustified claims to authority.[14]

Long before Foucalt, Matthew's gospel used genealogy in a similar way.[15] At first glance, Jesus' genealogy at the beginning of the gospel of Matthew looks like a traditionally structured Jewish family tree. Abraham, Isaac, Jacob and David all figure prominently, showing that Jesus was properly descended from his Jewish forefathers. But a closer look at the genealogy reveals the names of a number of women. This, in itself, was unusual for that day. But these women weren't just any women. They were the "skeletons in the closet" of the Biblical family.

You can almost see the shock when the name of Tamar is mentioned, bringing to mind the scandalous story of Genesis 28. Hands cover their ears when the names of the prostitute Rahab, and Ruth, the non-Jewish great grandmother of King David are read. The narrator continues, ignoring the discomfort, as they describe King Solomon's parentage as David and "the wife of Uriah," resurrecting the man whom David killed under the spell of his own libido. The final woman mentioned is, of course, Mary. The mother of Jesus became pregnant out of wedlock. These stories in the genealogy of Matthew's Savior protect the gospel from ideological entrapment. Injustice and oppression are acknowledged, not only in "the enemy's" genealogy, but in the Savior's as well. This prepares a level playing field for Matthew's gospel, the good news of God's forgiveness, grace, and love for everyone in Jesus Christ.

The Jesse Tree

Perhaps genealogy can have a similar effect on the story of Spanish Catholic Christianity in Los Angeles.

The genealogy of Los Angeles begins, of course, with the Native Americans who inhabited the region. It has long been known that Indian populations came to the Americas from Asia. recent DNA study suggests that Native American populations separated from Asian populations about 23,000 years ago before arriving on this continent about 13,000 years ago.[16]

The genealogy of many who represented the Spanish Empire in first contact with the Tongva bears surprising resemblance with the genealogy of the Native Americans. Carlos Francisco de Croix, for example, was the 55th Viceroy of Spain. But his origins are Flemish, not Spanish. Though often referred to as Carlos Francisco in the English listings of his name, his birth name was Francois Charles de Croix. He was born in the Flemish city of Lille, in today's Northern France. Not only did he grant permission for the Mission San Gabriel when he was Viceroy of New Spain from 1771-1776, but he is also credited with introducing French fashion and cuisine to the then capital of New Spain, Mexico City.

The Flemish people can be traced back to a tribe called the Menapii, who were part of a large federation of tribes that inhabited northern Gaul in pre-Roman and Roman times. Their land, which includes territory now in Belgium, France, and the Netherlands, was inhabited by the Menapii since the third century BC. But all of this would change, starting with Caesar conquering the Flemish in 57 BC. By the time the Viceroy was born and raised in Lille, they were under the rule of the Holy Roman Emperor Charles V. In 1688 the region became French. From 1708-1713 it was controlled by the Dutch. After the Viceroy's death, both Austria and England would attempt to gain control over the area. Like the Tongya, Carlos' heritage includes oppression and loss of land rights. Carlos Francisco isn't the only one with such a family tree.

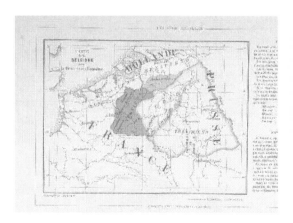

The Menapii Territory

Junipero Serra was born in Petra, Majorca. Majorca's original inhabitants moved to the island as early as 6,000 BC. Since then more than ten different groups have controlled the island: the Phoenicians in the eighth century BC, Rome in 123 BC, the Vandals in 427 AD, then the Byzantine Empire, the Muslim Emirate of Cordoba in 902, the Count of Barcelona in 1115, the North African Almoravides in 1176, the Almohad dynasty in 1229, the Kingdom of James I of Aragon in 1230, and finally Spain, which has remained in control of the island to the present day. Father Serra's DNA could easily include, not only Europeans, but Phoenicians, Vandals and North African parentage.

A Moorish Palace in Majorca

It isn't even clear whether Juan Rodriguez Cabrillo, who made first contact with the Tongva on October 8, 1542, was of Spanish heritage. He may have been Portuguese. But either way, he was every bit a part of the conquistador culture of this period.

In the 1490's two-way trade routes were developed across the Atlantic Ocean. This advance combined with a hunger for adventure and gave birth to the conquistador culture. Restall and Fernandez-Armesto describe the conquistadors as men who "went on their own initiative, assembling investors and companies of men with considerable individual effort and ingenuity. They were, in short, armed entrepreneurs."[17]

As a young man, Cabrillo joined forces with Hernan Cortez, conqueror of the Aztecs. Later Cabrillo became one of the wealthiest conquistadors by mining gold in Guatemala. Then, in Honduras, he became notorious for breaking up families of the natives by sending the men and boys into mines while giving the women and girls over to his soldiers and sailors. Some, at this point, might have rested with their spoils. But conquistadors continued to press forward in pursuit of additional wealth and social prestige. To turn back "assured debt, ignominy, and perhaps the retribution of a betrayed patron."[18] In 1540, Cabrillo sailed from Acajutla, El Salvador to Navidad, Mexico. This was the first leg of his voyage up the Pacific coast to find new opportunities for trade. On June 27, 1542, Cabrillo led three ships on the next leg of the journey, arriving in San Diego Bay about 3 months later. On the seventh of October he landed on Catalina Island and met, as described by the Spaniards, "a great crowd of armed Indians." These were the Tongva. The next day he landed at San Pedro Bay, the present-day site of the Port of Los Angeles, before continuing north in his search for trade.

In a Spanish report of that journey north of San Pedro Bay, we find that all was not well between the different tribes in the region. The Chumash called the Tatvian tribe in today's northwest Los Angeles County by the pejorative term "Alliklik," or grunters/stammers.[19] Another report says that the Xexo tribe in what is now Santa Barbara was ruled by an old woman. They were at war with the Xucu who lived in a region which is now part of Ventura County.

It wasn't until November 23, 1542 that Cabrillo returned to Catalina Island to winter and to make repairs. His contact with the area would quickly take an "L.A. turn." Just before Christmas Eve some of his men began fighting with the Tongva. Cabrillo ran from his ship to rescue them but stumbled on a jagged rock and splintered his shin. The injury became infected. He developed gangrene and then died on January 3, 1543. Cabrillo's dream of new trade routes was not fulfilled. The Spanish would return to the region, but not for another two centuries. They returned, not for trade, but to keep Russians from taking control of the region.

In 1741, the Russian explorer Vitus Bering made an expedition to Alaska. This was followed by an influx of Russian entrepreneurs who sought valuable furs from that region's harsh environment. The Russians continued their expeditions southward, eventually penetrating deep into California. King Carlos III, who considered these lands part of New Spain, became nervous. In 1766 he sent a Flemish soldier we already know, Francois Charles de Croix, as his personal representative to New Spain. His orders were to establish and maintain Spanish territorial integrity in California. Two years later, in 1768, there was a royal order which commanded the occupation of the Port of San Diego to prevent the Russians from taking control. "Spain would eventually have four presidios, twenty missions, and three pueblos" in California.[20] In 1770, 30 new friars were sent to California and Junipero Serra was chosen as the Superior of all of the "Alta California" missions. In 1771 Franciscan priests started the Mission San Gabriel Arcangel.

In many ways, it is amazing that the Spanish were able to colonize the area. At the time of the first European contact, the Tongva dominated this part of California; a region which covered 4,000 square miles. They were part of a sophisticated network of trading partners that included the Chumash to the west, the Cahuilla and Mojave to the east, and the Juaneños and Luiseños to the south. Their trade, which included slavery, extended all the way to the Colorado River.[21] The number of Spanish personnel who were involved in this colonization, on the other hand, was minimal.

> At the outset only a couple of hundred men arrived. Another three or four hundred men, women and children came in the next dozen years ... Even in 1821 they and their descendants, the genre de razon (the Spanish culture bearers) were only a very few thousand, far outnumbered by the missionized Indians then approaching 20,000.[22]

Carlos Francisco used the standard frontier institutions of late colonial Spain in his task: the presidio, the mission and the pueblo. The presidio was a garrisoned fort which housed soldiers. The mission was a community which, though led by Catholic fathers, was a predominantly Indian community whose goal was to become self-supporting and to induct the Native Americans into

Spanish culture. The pueblo was a civilian town. In order to succeed, this system required a working relationship between the Native Americans and the Spanish. The system near Los Angeles depended greatly on the presence of the prosperous Tongva village of Yang-Na. The village on the banks of the Los Angeles River was originally inhabited in the 1500s. In 1542 Cabrillo actually noted the village on his map of the area. Over 200 years later, in 1769, a Spanish army captain, Gaspar de Portola, and a priest named Juan Crespi, arrived on their way to Monterrey Bay. Crespi made an entry in his diary about Yang-Na calling it the most delightful place he had ever been. The Spanish pueblo for this area developed next to the village. The Tongva and the colonists worked together to develop a water system. The two communities built a dam made of sand and willow poles about two miles northeast of the area. They also worked together on zanjas or ditches which would bring the water to the colony. The Zanja Madre or mother ditch, parts of which have been rediscovered recently in Los Angeles, was completed in October 1781 and became a major source of water for the growing community.[23] The village of Yang-Na also provided the colonists with seafood, fish, bowls, pelts and baskets. It was common for the Native Americans and the colonists to intermarry. Eventually the Tongva became known by association with two missions in the area: the Gabrieleños (for their connection to the San Gabriel Mission), and the Fernandeños (who were connected to the San Fernando Mission).

Before the arrival of the Padres, the Tongva were governed by a set of religious and cultural practices that included belief in creative supernatural forces. According to Kroeber,[24] the pre-Christian Tongva had a "mythic-ritual-social six-god pantheon." They believed they were ruled over by the god Weywot. He was a cruel task master who was eventually killed by his own sons. When the Tongva assembled to decide what to do next, they had a vision of a ghostly being who called himself Quaoar. He told them that he had come to restore order and to give laws to the people. After giving instructions regarding which groups would have political and spiritual leadership, he began to dance. Then he slowly ascended into heaven. Some of their beliefs had parallels in Christianity. For example, their Great Morning Ceremony was based on a belief in the afterlife. They also had a purification ritual with similarities to the Christian Eucharist or Lord's Supper.

With the arrival of Portola's caravan in 1776, these religious parallels between the two faiths, as well as their differences, would become clear. Pedro Font, a member of that Portola's caravan which arrived in the area in 1776, kept a journal. In it he described the ministry of the Missions in a way which reveals the intermingling of Christianity and Spanish colonization:

> The method which the fathers observe in the conversion is not to oblige anyone to become a Christian, admitting only those who voluntarily offer themselves, and this they do in the following manner: Since the Indians are accustomed to live in the fields and the hills like beasts, the fathers require that if they wish to be Christians they shall no longer go to the forest, but must live in the mission; and if they leave the rancheria, as they call the little village of huts and houses of the Indians, they will go to seek them and will punish them. With this they begin to catechize the heathen who voluntarily come, teaching them to make the sign of the cross and other things necessary, and if they persevere in the catechism for two or three months and in the same frame of mind, when they are instructed they proceed to baptize them. If any Indian wishes to go to the mountain to see his relatives or to hunt acorns, they give him permission for a specified number of days. As a rule, they do not fail to return, and sometimes they come bringing some heathen relative, who remains for the catechism, either through the example of the others or attracted by the pozole (porridge), which they like better than

their herbs and the foods of the mountain; and so these Indians are usually caught by the mouth.[25]

Despite the distortions of the gospel, which we see in this description, the Missions in Alta California had quite a bit of short term success. By 1820, 20,000 Indians were part of the Mission system which was led by 26 missionaries. It also must be said that many of the Spanish Missionaries "believed it to be their duty to safeguard the Indians from exploitation by the settlers, to prevent them from being enslaved, and to provide them with religious instruction and clerical ministrations."[26] But the conquistadores who came to the new world "considered it beneath their dignity to soil their hands with spade, plough or pick."[27] Most of those who crossed the Atlantic did so, not for the welfare of the Indians, but to accumulate wealth.

The friction between these two views in Spanish culture became apparent as early as the 1500's. It was during this time that Prior Bernardino de Minaya in the Caribbean island of Hispaniola wrote letters to the Pope warning of the abuses being perpetrated against the Indians. In response, the Pope issued a formal decree, or Papal Bull, stating that "the said Indians and all other peoples who hereafter shall be brought to notice of Catholics, although they may be without faith in Jesus Christ, in no wise are they to be deprived of their liberty and of the control of their goods; in no wise are they to be made slaves."[28]

Regardless of the Papal decree, the abuses continued. The Valladolid debate was called. This would be the first moral debate in Europe on the rights and treatment of the colonized people in the Americas. From 1550-1551 people of opposing views debated issues such as the justification for the conversion of the Native Americans to Catholicism, the way the colonized were to be integrated into colonial life, and Native American rights and obligations. French historian Jean Dumont sees this debate as a major turning point in world history. "In that moment in Spain appeared the dawn of human rights."[29]

In 1573 King Phillip II signed the Law of the Indies which included 148 ordinances to guide those who were locating, building, and popularizing settlements in the new world. These laws were heavily influenced by Vitruvius' Ten Books of Architecture, written before the first century A.D. and Leon Battista Alberti's works from the 15th century. Like the Papal Bull more than 60 years before, these laws forbade the enslaving of Indians. Specifically, the leaders of the colony, the Encomendero, were responsible to see that the Indians under their care were treated as free people, that they were given non-hazardous labor in proportion to their strength, that they were paid for their labor with wages adequate to support themselves and their families, and that they were given Christian instruction. But distance and the politics in Spain proved more powerful than the Law of the Indies. As one critic put it, "Christianity, instead of fulfilling its mission of enlightening, converting and sanctifying the natives, was itself converted; Paganism was baptized; Christianity was paganized."[30]

Conquistador culture began a steep decline. Spain had become "stuck." Historian, Ricardo Garcia Carcel described the internal dysfunction of Spain in the twilight years of conquistador culture: "Spain became a nation of perplexed and ill-defined people, engulfed by political and social crisis."[31] Carcel made these comments at a conference of Don Quixote related seminars meeting in Valladolid, where the author of Don Quixote, Miguel de Cervantes Saavedra, had once lived. Cervantes wrote at a time Spaniards were struggling to survive "a shapeless and threatening social order, while the imperial court still imposed its rigid customs and morals." His book satirized conquistador culture.

> Destiny guides our fortunes more favorably than we could
> have expected. Look there, Sancho Panza, my friend, and see
> those thirty or so wild giants, with whom I intend to do battle
> and kill each and all of them, so with their stolen booty we
> can begin to enrich ourselves. This is noble, righteous

warfare, for it is wonderfully useful to God to have such an evil race wiped from the face of the earth." "What giants?" Asked Sancho Panza. "The ones you can see over there," answered his master, "with the huge arms, some of which are very nearly two leagues long." "Now look, your grace," said Sancho, "what you see over there aren't giants, but windmills, and what seems to be arms are just their sails, that go around in the wind and turn the millstone." "Obviously," replied Don Quixote, "you don't know much about adventures.[32]

His book reflected the gulf between appearance and reality in Spain at this time of change. "Like the student idealists of 1968," Carcel said, "Cervantes' twin heroes take their dreams for reality and believe in the reality of their dreams."[33]

In few decaying empires," says Dr. Dillon, "is the contrast between the glorious past and the sordid present, between fantastic dreams and repulsive facts, splendid possibilities and hateful realities, so striking and so cruel as in the land of Cervantes, Cortes, and Calderon de la Barca. That once mighty kingdom is now but the nearest shadow of its former self.[34]

The collapse of the Mission system in Los Angeles quickly followed.

Once Mexico gained independence from Spain, the Missions were secularized, their land was taken, and the buildings themselves fell into disrepair. The Native Americans were no longer being groomed as Spanish citizens. Christianity's influence among the Native Americans dissipated rapidly as well. The Missions themselves were not viewed with admiration in L.A. during this chapter in the city's history.

The Catholic Church, however, did raise up the lives of the Mission fathers, including Junipero Serra, as examples for the faithful to follow.[35] Hagiography is a literary form that predates modern history. It is, in fact, a mistake to equate hagiography and history because hagiography is a kind of narrative used for a particular purpose, not only by Christianity, but by other religions as well.[36] Thus they emphasize the miraculous deeds of the saints in a way that goes far beyond the experience of the reader. Hagiography isn't written just to "tell it as it happens." It isn't even written to promote Spanish colonization. The goal of these stories is to encourage the faithful by idealizing the saints' heroic actions through their common faith in God. They were meant to encourage other Catholics to live heroic lives in their own situation.

Another genre of the Mission story emerged with a more earthly goal in mind. "Mission Romances," like hagiography, weren't written as history. But neither were they written to encourage the Catholic faithful. The Romances, motivated by real estate interests in Los Angeles, "rebooted" the stories of the "Mission way of life" to draw more people to the city of Los Angeles. John O. Pohlman, in "California's Mission Myth" writes,

> For people concerned about the image of southern California's stability and its permanent development, what better tactic could have been devised than to create and project the appearance of security by enthusiastically emphasizing supposedly long-standing traditions--cultural, agricultural, architectural, educational, spiritual and hospitable? As early as 1893 the first of many books popularizing the mission romance for tourists contended that preservation of the Franciscan missions would provide evidence of California's stability.[37]

John Steven McGoarty's "Mission Play" grew out of the Mission Romances. In language which reflects Cervantes, but without any sense of irony, the Mission Play describe how the Fathers "took an idle race and put it to work-- a useless race that they made useful in the world, a naked race and they clothed it, a hungry race and they lifted it up into the great white glory of God."[38]

It is worth considering whether the backlash in response to the Pope's visit in the 21st century wasn't motivated, at least in part, by the portrayal of this way of life in the Mission Romances. Could at least part of the target of modern revisionist history be the real estate interests of the 19th and early 20th century?

The stories of the Mission Romances are a far cry from the intentions of Spanish-Mission Catholicism. For all of its failings, the Missions represented a holistic attempt to integrate outsiders into the dominant Spanish Christian world. Though there are many reasons to criticize the approach of the Padres, their motivation of sharing a way of life that they themselves have found deeply meaningful stands in stark contrast, not only to the motives of the authors of the Mission Romances, but to the systems of oppression and slavery of Spanish colonization.

Perhaps a word from Gertrude Himmelfarb could be helpful here. In "The New History and the Old," she writes that there is a way of looking at the past which:

> denies to the past an integrity and will of its own, in which people acted out of a variety of motives, and in which events had a multiplicity of causes. It imposes upon the past the same determinism that it imposes upon the present, thus robbing people of their individuality and events of their complexity.[39]

From the perspective of Christian mission, Spanish-Mission Catholicism ultimately failed. Not only did it fail to prevent systematic oppression of the Native Americans by the Spanish, but it also failed to transmit effectively the message of the forgiveness, grace and love of God in Christ to the Native American people in any lasting way.

This assessment highlights a recurring theme in Christianity that can help Los Angeles build a new, more united, identity. Human history shows repeatedly that we are simply unable to construct a way of life which guarantees the kind of city we all desire to live in. The "skeletons in the closet" of Los Angeles' genealogy show this to be true of Los Angeles as well. This theme gives rise to such phrases from the New Testament as, "For all have sinned and fallen short of the glory of God" and "There is no one righteous, not even one." Properly understood within Christianity, these words disarm any theology or ideology which promotes one group of humans over another by placing us all together on a "level playing field." It is from this vantage point of our common inability to create the way of life we desire that we can find a new beginning.

A more united identity for the city emerges from the assessment of the Mission system by a Presbyterian minister in Los Angeles in the 1920's.

> Some writers have described their founders as saints and heroes, who combined in themselves all virtues, powers and graces. Others have represented them as being mere slave drivers, who employed low cunning in exploiting the Indians and who were quite unworthy of the name Christian. It is very certain that no extreme estimate is a true one. On the whole the Padres would seem to have been very human, and their defects to have been largely those of the system of which they were a part.[40]

If Angelenos look at the past and present of Los Angeles from a similar perspective, they will find that this genealogy, skeletons and all, has the ability to reveal a common identity for the city. This isn't just theory or theology. This is reality. A reality that goes "bone deep."

The 2007 census of L.A., for example, shows that Native Americans continue to have a strong presence in the city. 146,500 Native Americans live in Los Angeles, the largest Native American population of any city in the United States. But we cannot forget that Native Americans are also represented in the DNA of the "Hispanic/Latino" designation in the census.

Hispanic refers to Spanish-speaking people while Latino refers to people of Latin American descent. This grouping makes up 47.9% of the city, the largest designation of any demographic in L.A. Latin American people are a mix of European (primarily Spanish), African and Native American peoples. This largest demographic, then, represents, not only the Spanish, but Native Americans as well. The City of Angels of the 21st century is irreducibly the result of this chapter between the Spanish and the Native Americans in Los Angeles' family history. What would it mean for Angelenos to embrace this reality?

Momondo.com is a Copenhagen based travel metasearch engine that enables its users to find and compare prices of travel products. Launched in 2006, their search engine is multilingual allowing searches in Danish, Swedish, Norwegian, Finnish, Polish, Ukrainian, Chinese, English, German, French, Spanish, Portuguese, Italian, Russian, Dutch and Turkish. They set up a contest in which 67 people would be chosen to take a DNA test and then, depending on their DNA results, from the results, are provided with free trips to visit their "homeland." In watching promotional videos of some of the winners, it is clear that Momondo touched on something more important than their travel business.

Carlos saw himself as 100% Cuban. His greatest fear about the DNA test would be finding out that he is Dominican. He wasn't going to be happy with any Argentinian or French DNA either. "Whatever is in there you will still be Carlos, right?" He was clearly nervous about receiving his DNA results. The researcher was trying to comfort him.

When he opened his results, Carlos found that 22% of his DNA was from Spain/Portugal. 17% was Native American. 16% was south eastern African. 12% was from Italy and Greece. He also had DNA from Niger, Great Britain, Senegal, Ivory Coast/Ghana, Benin/Togo, Mali, Eastern Europe, the Middle East, Cameroon/Togo, Scandinavia and Melanesia. Carlos had the most varied DNA the researchers had ever seen. His response? "This is really unbelievable!" "I am a real man of the world."[41]

Let us hope that Los Angeles will choose the same response to its genealogy. Such an approach will enable the city to embrace one of its most amazing qualities: its diversity. For L.A., like few other cities, brings Martin Luther King Jr.'s word to life: We are caught in an inescapable mutuality. Whatever effects one directly, affects all indirectly. All life is interrelated.[42]

Chapter 7

Melchizedek in L.A.

For the Glory of the Lord
Following the example of Abraham
The Father of the Faith, and of the
Pilgrims who preceded us to
This Land, we have built an altar
And dedicate it to God with
Unspeakable gratitude. May our
Posterity also be a peculiar
People to Bless mankind.
-Berendo Street Korean Baptist Church[1]

Every Sunday in Los Angeles you can hear Angelenos worshipping Jesus in English and Spanish, in Korean and Japanese, in Persian and Armenian. Every day the embodiment of the ancient Christian vision statement in the book of Acts is on display for all to see: 'But you will receive power when the Holy Spirit comes on you; and you will be my witnesses in Jerusalem, and in all Judea and Samaria, and to the ends of the earth.' Surely, given the cross-racial reach of this once Jewish sect, Christianity can help the City of Angels find a narrative which embraces its own rich multi-ethnicity.

Like the city, the church in the United States has struggled with its multicultural character. Martin Luther King Jr., in a "Meet the Press" interview in 1960, pointed out that Sunday is the most segregated day of the week. This statement rightly shamed the American church for its reinforcement of the racial divisions so prevalent in the United States. The church is meant to be a model, not a mirror for the nation in which it finds itself. To assume, however, that the goal of Christianity is one worship service, in one language, under one denominational structure, for all people misses King Jr.'s point. It also misunderstands the nature of Christian unity. For Christianity, like Los Angeles, has been varied and diverse in expression of its faith since its early days. The Christian mandate is not to uniformity. It is, instead, to live and worship in a way which transcends the social boundaries in which it finds itself. This was surely King's point in 1960.

It is this mandate which has the potential to help Los Angeles embrace its multicultural character in a way that transcends the ideological, economic, linguistic, and cultural boundaries which have limited and segmented the city. Conformity is not the means by which Christianity heals the wounds caused by human difference. In the New Testament reversal of the ancient story of the Tower of Babel, people of different cultural influences were unified, not by a common language, but by a common vision of life translated into multiple languages.[3] Unity in Los Angeles, like unity in Christ, should never mean that everyone thinks, acts or speaks in the same way. Los Angeles has too much life, too much diversity and far too much creativity for such a limited vision. Unity in Los Angeles is a unity in diversity.

Thus far in its history, Los Angeles has been unable to develop a narrative which encompasses its rich diversity. The Mission system's attempts to assimilate Native Americans into Spanish Catholic culture gave way to the idea of the melting pot. The melting pot has given way to ideas like multiculturalism and identity politics in attempts to embrace the diversity of the city. To date these approaches have had a limited impact. The city is still divided. But, as we saw in the previous chapter, there is a deeper story going on in the communities of L.A. Underneath the clash between the Europeans and Native Americans, beyond the very real struggle of African-Americans with Caucasian privilege there are millions of people living their lives in thousands of relational networks in the City of Angels. As Pico Iyer wrote in the late 20th century, Los Angeles is a city with:

> more Thais than any city but Bangkok, more Koreans than any city but Seoul, more El Salvadorans than any city outside of San Salvador, more Druze than anywhere but Beirut . . . the easternmost outpost of Asia and the northernmost province of Mexico."[4]

To put it simply, L.A. needs a more inclusive narrative which reflects and inspires its real identity; a way of being that is even more complicated and varied than our ideological descriptions allow.

Some Ethnic Enclaves in Los Angeles

Los Angeles' true identity can be found with a look at the Los Angeles census. In 2007 the L.A. census consisted of 5 major racial/cultural demographics:

47.9% Hispanic/Latino

27.5% White, Non-Hispanic

13.7% Asian/Pacific Islander

8.1% African American

2.8% American Indian/Other

At first glance, the census supports the history popularly told. The Native Americans were the first to inhabit the land. They were at peace until the arrival of the Spanish colonizers who overwhelmed the Native Americans and took their land. That is why, we are told, we have only 2.8% American Indian/Other while we have 47.9% Hispanic/Latino and 27.5% White, Non-Hispanics. But can it be that over 75% of the present population comes from the colonizers?

We have already noted that American Indian DNA is also represented in the Hispanic/Latino category since many Latinos are a mixture of Native American, Spanish and African ethnicity. This also means that African DNA is represented in this category as well as in the "African-American" category.

We find a similar overlap with the "Asian/Pacific Islander" and the "White, non-Hispanic" categories of the census. Koreans and Japanese have been grouped together with Chinese and Filipinos in the "Asian-Pacific Islander" grouping. Such designations lock them in definitions which actually do violence to their self-understanding. Koreans are, as Rieff put it, "lumped in the same category as their country's hated traditional master, the Japanese."[5] There are similar concerns with the white/non-Hispanic category. This designation, according to the Los Angeles Census of 2016, is for "A person having origins in any of the original peoples in Europe, North Africa or the Middle East." Armenians and Turks are counted together with those of Persian heritage. Again, as David Rieff put it, "In the space of three generations or less, immigrants would move from being part of a subgroup within their own countries of origins to becoming an American minority group... In El Salvador you were not a Hispanic, you were Salvadoran. In Asia you were not Asian, you were Chinese. And yet in Los Angeles, these deepest of selves were simply subsumed in the broader context of a new, overarching Hispanicity or Asianness."[6] The census may support the narratives built around Western agendas, but this blurring of ethnic and cultural distinctions makes it difficult to see the stories of the many people ignored by such tales. The stories of the Koreans and Japanese and the Armenians and Persians cannot be heard for their own contributions. But L.A. needs these very stories if the city is going to develop a way for all of its inhabitants to move forward together.

The Armenians, for example, are a people with a long cultural and religious tradition. The third largest diaspora community of Armenians in the entire world have made Los Angeles their home. Their story as a people takes us to a time more than 1,500-years before first contact between the Tongva and the Spanish. It tells of St. Thaddeus, also known as Jude in the New Testament, making first Christian contact with the Armenians in AD 43. St. Bartholomew, another Apostle of the New Testament, followed in AD 66.

Both were martyred. But they paved the way, three centuries later, for St. Gregory the Illuminator who played a key role in the conversion of the Armenian people to Christianity. All of this occurred well before the Tongva started the settlement of Yang Na. Then, in 405 AD, Mesrop Mashtots invented the Armenian alphabet and completed the first Armenian translation of the Bible. Today the Armenian people hold a place of honor in Christian history. As Aram Yeretzian points out: "The Armenian Gregorian Church was the first national church, and the Armenians were the first people who accepted Christianity as the national faith."[7] Since that time, through generations of life in diaspora communities, "The Armenian Church has held the race together."[8] The Armenians first arrived in Los Angeles in 1899. And yet, their story has yet to be fully integrated into the popular narrative of the city.

And their story is only the first of many. L.A. is also home to the largest population of Persians of any city outside of Iran. Persians are a people with an ancient story that has significant overlap with the Armenian story (see below). Greater L.A. is home to the largest Korean population of any city in the United States. The City of Angels is second only to Honolulu in the number of Japanese living within city bounds. To understand Los Angeles and Christianity in Los Angeles we must find a narrative for the city that invites these voices to shape the story of L.A.

Engaging those who are outside of the common narrative starts at the same place in any city or time. Dr. Jehu Hanciles reminds us that, "In all cultural interactions, people interpret and appropriate new concepts and experiences in terms of preexisting views and values."[9] And yet, there are moments when an outside voice breaks through and actually becomes part of the prevailing narrative. Los Angeles needs such moments. The biblical story of Melchizedek demonstrates how this might happen.

In Genesis 14, right in the middle of the narrative of Abraham's quest for the Jewish Promised Land, a stranger appears out of nowhere. His background is completely unknown to the narrative yet he comes to play a key role in the story.

> Then Melchizedek king of Salem brought out bread and wine.
> He was priest of God Most High, and he blessed Abram, saying,
> 'Blessed be Abram by God Most High,
>   Creator of heaven and earth.
> And praise be to God Most High,
>   who delivered your enemies into your hand.'
> Then Abraham gave him a tenth of everything. -Genesis 14:18-20

This story of Abraham story could flow on its own without Melchizedek. Here is how it would read without him in the narrative:

> After Abram returned from defeating Kedorlaomer and the kings allied with him, the king of Sodom came out to meet him in the Valley of Shaveh (that is, the King's Valley)." "The king of Sodom said to Abram, 'Give me the people and keep the goods for yourself. -Genesis 14:17, 21

But in between these two sentences we have the story of Melchizedek. His appearance actually disrupts the narrative. This is the next step in hearing other voices in the narrative of Los Angeles. But for a new narrative to develop out of such an event, at least three more things need to happen. The prevailing narrative needs to acknowledge its own limitations in light of this other voice. These new possibilities allow the narrative to grow in unexpected directions. And then the new possibilities are then enabled to grow in directions which are not under the previous narrative's control.

An Early Mosaic Depicting Melchizedek

Melchizedek represents a story that is much older than the narrative of Abraham in Genesis. Melchizedek's moniker, "the King of Salem" (v.18) identifies him as the king of ancient Jerusalem.[10] This man was king of that city long before Israel established it as the City of David. Melchizedek also represents an older faith in the God of Israel. Abraham had only recently moved from his syncretistic ancestral beliefs toward the monotheism of Judaism.[11] But, as "Priest of the Most High God," Melchizedek was part of a priesthood that the Jewish people had not yet developed. It takes humility to give voice to such an advanced character from outside of your story. Los Angeles needs this kind of humility.

The Armenians, Japanese, Koreans and Iranians provide Los Angeles with just such an opportunity. For though they enter the story of Los Angeles after the chapter of the Native Americans and the Spaniards, they represent cultures which are much more ancient. Japanese history goes back thousands of years. But they began to arrive in Southern California in the 1890s due to anti-Asian sentiment in San Francisco. The first Korean Presbyterian Church in Los Angeles was established in this city in 1905. But the Koreans already had a history of conflict with the Japanese when Cabrillo landed in San Pedro Bay. The vast majority of Persians are even more recent arrivals to Los Angeles than the Japanese, Koreans and Armenians. Most arrived after the Iranian Revolution of 1979. But 2,000 years before U.S. independence they were a great empire. All of these people, like Melchizedek in Genesis, represent a much more ancient history than Los Angeles. All of them have something to teach the city.

Persia held sway over an empire of 5.5 million square kilometers, almost 75% of the size of the contiguous United States, from 550 to 330 BC in what is known as the Achaemid Empire. It was the largest empire of its time covering a region including parts of Greece, Libya and Egypt to the west across Turkey, Israel and Iraq to Afghanistan, Pakistan and parts of present day India in the east. This empire had a direct impact on the Armenians. The Greek historian Herodotus (484-425 BC) writes about the Armenians crossing into their homeland around 1000 BC. Centuries later, when Cyrus the Great, founder of the Achaemid Empire, conquered lands which included the Armenian homeland, it brought an era of peace to the region which is even celebrated in the Bible.[12]

At the time of the Persian Empire under Cyrus, Buddhism was being introduced into classical Japan by King Seong starting a new chapter in that country's history which traces back as far as 10,000 BC. King Seong's Kingdom, called Baekje, was founded in 18 BC and eventually became one of the three kingdoms of Korea.

It isn't just the city of Los Angeles that needs to learn humility in the face of these ancient narratives. The Christian churches in L.A. need more respect as well. Christianity was introduced in the Armenian and Persian narratives long before the history of Christianity in Alta California. Their interaction with Christianity predates the Protestant Reformation. It was being written well before the development of the Roman Catholic Church.

An Armenian Archbishop in the 19th Century

The Armenians have preserved the ancient story of how their people became Christian. On his way to Armenia to claim his throne, Drtad III met Gregory, son of Anak. Impressed with his abilities, the King brought him to Armenia. When Gregory, who had earlier become a Christian, refused to participate in pagan rituals and honor the goddess Anahit, the pagan Drtad III ordered him thrown into a deep pit full of snakes. Gregory remained there for years. When Drtad III became seriously ill, his sister Khosrovitoukht had a dream that only Gregory could save the king. She summoned Gregory, who had somehow survived, and he cured the king. Now convinced that Gregory's faith was the true one, Drtad III converted to Christianity in AD 301, making Armenia the first Christian nation. Gregory became known as Gregory the Illuminator.[13]

The story of Christianity's origins among the Persians goes back to Saba (died AD 487) who was born in Media, Iran to an aristocratic family. His father was Zoroastrian but his mother hired a Christian nurse to raise him. He later attended Christian school. He grew to be a committed Christian, distributing his property among the poor, persuading his mother to be baptized, and then retiring to a monastery. He and a colleague engaged in mission work, convincing an entire city, including its Zoroastrian priest, to become Christian. They also brought some Kurdish people in the region to faith in Christ.[14]

A 17th Century Persian Christian Bishop

If the popular narratives of Los Angeles and of Christianity in Los Angeles can acknowledge their limitations in light of the much more ancient stories among those who now call L.A. home, and allow those narratives to disrupt their own, they may be able to find new possibilities for their own narrative which has become stuck. This is what happens to the biblical narrative under the influence of Melchizedek.

The King of Sodom, in verse 21, has been humbled through defeat in battle. Abraham had been drawn into this battle because of family responsibility. His nephew, Lot, lived in Sodom. The threat on that city, then, became a threat to Abraham's family. Abraham's victory saved the King's throne as well. The King of Sodom said to Abraham, "Give me the people and keep the goods for yourself." In contrast, Mechizedek, who seems to have escaped the conflict, comes with bread and wine and offers Abraham a blessing from God. Abraham rejects the offer of the King of Sodom and accepts Melchizidek's blessing. His tribute to Melchizedek decisively turns the narrative from a story of the military history of the patriarch Abraham to a spiritual story of the people of God.

Surely the stories of these more recent immigrants could transform the narrative of Los Angeles in such a decisive way. For example, the Iranians, Armenians, Japanese and Koreans came to L.A. in search of a place of stability in the midst of cultural and religious turmoil. This continues the theme of a dream developed elsewhere but pursued in the city. It shifts the present mode of this theme from the individual quest for self-fulfillment to social/familial networks seeking a place to live in peace.

The Iranians arrived in Los Angeles in two major waves. The first from 1950-1977 when 35,000 Persian immigrants arrived in the city. The second, much larger wave, was between 1978 and 1986 in the wake of the Islamic Revolution which overthrew the Pahlavi dynasty (1925-1979).[15] Like the migration of the Armenians, the Iranian migration to the United States was not the first mass migration in the country's long history. As Ron Kelley writes in *Irangeles: Iranians in Los Angeles:*

> The history of exile in Iran goes back at least to the eighth century, when a group of Persian Zoroastrians in search of religious freedom left Iran to form their own community in India. Since then, Persians have frequently migrated to escape religious persecution and political oppression or to seek economic opportunities.[16]

The 1979 revolution in Iran overthrew the Persian monarchy which had been in continuous rule for 2,500 years. This dramatic change in governance pushed a particular demographic out of Iran and to Los Angeles. This group is highly educated, professional, and entrepreneurial, and many fled from the capital of Iran.[17] Though they are from a common strata of society, the Iranians in Los Angeles are socially and religiously diverse. They include Shi'i Muslim Iranians, Armenian Iranians, Jewish Iranians, Kurdish Iranians, as well as Zoroastrians, Assyrians and Bahai. Their lives in Los Angeles have tended "to reinforce internal ethnicity rather than an encompassing Iranian nationality."[18] The Iranian Jews tend to live in downtown Los Angeles. The Armenian Iranians live with other Armenians in Glendale. The Bahai and the Muslims, and others congregate in Little Tehran. On Westwood Boulevard just south of Westwood Village, Persian script appears on storefronts, and from Iranian restaurants the distinctive aromas of Persian cuisine permeate the air. Although they have made their home in Los Angeles, the Persians who live in L.A. are, for the most part, a people in exile, ready to return to Iran if there is a favorable change of government.

Like the Iranians, the Armenians in Los Angeles share a history of exile. Armenians had their own country with civil and political institutions by 565 BC.[19] In 67 BC they became an ally of Rome, eventually losing their independence and becoming, instead, a tributary of the Roman Empire. In AD 1375 many were absorbed into the rapidly rising Turkish Empire although significant populations of Armenians had migrated to Iran and Russia. When the Ottoman Empire began to decline, the prejudice against the Armenians grew. One story of their experience should suffice.

> In June 1893, four young Armenians and their wives went out from their village homes about two miles from Van where the governor resides with a large military force and were picking herbs together on a hillside. They knew the perils of the land and kept close together. A band of Kurds passing by in broad daylight was attracted by the appearance of the young women, fell upon the little party, butchered the young men, outraged the young brides, mounted their horses and rode away. The next day the villagers brought in the four bodies, slashed and disfigured. Yoking up four rude ox carts they placed on each the naked remains of one of the victims with his widow sitting by his side, her hair shorn off in token of her dishonor. The village folk marched along with the carts in gruesome procession to the city. They bared their breasts to the bayonets of the Turkish soldiers who tried to turn them back and marched on through the streets of the city, multitudes of Armenians joining them and moving without tumult. The procession passed before the doors of the British and Russian Vice-Consulates, of the Persian Consul-General,

the Chief of Police and other high officials, till it paused before the great palace of the Governor. The Governor looked out of the window and said: 'I see it. Too bad! Take them away and bury them. I will do what is necessary.' Within two days some Kurds were brought in, among whom were several who were positively identified by the women, but, upon their denying the crime, they were immediately released. Later the Governor went out to the scene of the outrage and finding that an Armenian monastery was the nearest inhabited building, accused the priest of the murder, pillaged the monastery and punished the venerable old man at its head. This incident is not exceptional. It is illustrative of what was going on somewhere among the Armenians all the time.[20]

Armenian Refugees About 1899

Not only were the Armenians victimized in the 19th century, but they were slaughtered by the Turks after World War I. Armenians in Russia suffered during the Stalinist purges from 1936-1938 resulting in waves of immigration to the US beginning in 1940. These waves continued, especially after the US Immigration and Nationality Act of 1965 changed the US system of immigration which had discriminated against non-northern Europeans. In the 1970s and 1980s, 80,000 more Armenians arrived in the United States, some from Lebanon after the 1975 civil war, others after the 1988 earthquake in Armenia which killed between 25,000 and 50,000 people.[21]

The Armenians typically live in communities with other Armenians in Los Angeles. One of the largest communities of Armenians in Los Angeles is in the city of Glendale. Glendale dramatically changed when Armenian Iranians joined earlier Armenian immigrants from other lands (Armenia and Russia, for example). There was some upset among city residents when these new immigrants paid cash for up-scale homes and businesses in the area. Real estate prices soared. But the city has adapted. Though Armenians in Los Angeles are still strongly defined by their nationality and Christian faith,[22] they have put down deep roots in L.A.

Unlike Persians and Armenians, the Korean exodus of 1903-1905 was the first in that country's official history. "Koreans were land-bound and lived immobile in an agrarian society, imbued with Confucian values that regarded leaving their ancestors' tombs as a crime--let alone a trans-Pacific migration to an utterly unknown land."[23] But events would force the hermit kingdom to open up to the rest of the world.

In 1866, 21 years after Korea put one of their own to death for 'communicating with Western barbarians,' an American schooner called 'Surprise', wrecked on the Korean coast. The crew were treated hospitably, supplied with food and clothing, and sent on their way. In the fall a merchant schooner, the 'General Sherman,' sailed up the Ta-tong River ostensibly for trade, but under circumstances which aroused suspicion. Its crew soon got into difficulties with the people and were killed, while the ship was totally destroyed.[24]

Then, in 1871 an armed expedition was sent to negotiate a treaty after a "piratical expedition to pilfer the royal tombs of Korea" failed. This expedition didn't go well either and 3 Americans and 400 Koreans died. This reinforced Korean attitudes toward the "Western barbarians."[25]

In the 19th century Korea slowly disintegrated. The Sino-Japanese War in 1884 and the Russo-Japanese rivalry forced Korea into a national crisis. Many Koreans were forced to consider Immigration to Hawaii as "the only answer to the prevailing economic and political situation."[26]

On January 13, 1903, 101 Korean immigrants arrived by ship in Honolulu to be sugar cane farm laborers. By 1905 there were 7,000 Koreans in Hawaii. In the same year, the Korean community in Los Angeles began to develop with the organization of the first Korean Presbyterian Church near the USC campus on Jefferson Boulevard. More Koreans arrived in the 1930s with approximately 650 forming a community in what is now South Central Los Angeles. Then, the Korean War of 1950-53 caused another wave of Korean immigration to the United States. By 1964 this wave had brought another 14,000 Koreans. Between 1965 and 1980 some 299,000 Koreans immigrated to the United States. "Los Angeles has become the largest port of entry for the new Korean immigrants and home of the largest such community in the country."[27]

The Japanese came to the city, as mentioned earlier, in the 1890's after they suffered persecution, not in Japan, but in San Francisco. By December 1941 there were 37,000 ethnic Japanese in Los Angeles County. After Pearl Harbor many of these families were "evacuated" to special camps according to Executive Order 9066 issued by President Roosevelt. After the war many of these families returned to the Boyle Heights neighborhood in L.A.

All of these people have come to Los Angeles in pursuit of a dream, but a different kind of dream than those considered in earlier chapters. They share the dream of persecuted and exiled people around the world. They are looking for a city where they might simply be free to live, work and raise a family in peace. Though it is a narrative held by many Angelenos, it has yet to impact the popular narrative of Los Angeles.

However, these immigrant Angelenos are already changing Los Angeles. Allowing these stories a voice will turn the narrative of Los Angeles in directions which are not under control of the official narratives. We can't say what that will look like, but there are already a number of clues.

One of these clues is the term "transmigrant." The description, developed by Nina Glick Schiller, describes people with multiple social relations of both origin and residence, people like many of the people we have discussed in this chapter. "Transmigrants are often bilingual, able to lead dual lives, move easily between cultures, frequently maintain a home in two countries, and are incorporated as social actors in both...their communities remain ethnically distinguishable regardless of acculturation."[28] According to Alejandro Portes, transmigration has led "to the diminishing likelihood of uniform processes of assimilation and rapid integration in Western society."[29]

Another clue surfaced in the most recent riots in Los Angeles. The popular narrative of the riots following the arrest of Rodney King tells of the conflict between Caucasians and African-Americans. But the reality is more complex. There is substantial evidence that the relationship between African-Americans and Koreans, and even Latino gang members is a key part of this story. We have already mentioned the Latasha Harlins case (chapter 5) which, according to UCLA historian Brenda Stevenson, caused a great rise in tensions before the riots. This thesis is supported by the focus of destruction during the riots. Forty-one Korean owned businesses were torched and dozens more were looted in the riots in South Central Los Angeles.[30] CNN reported a dramatic story entitled, "The LA riots were a rude awakening for Korean-Americans," which illustrates this angle of the story. "Chang Lee gripped his fingers tighter around the gun and screamed at potential looters from the rooftop of the small strip mall where he stood. The 35-year-old had never held a firearm before the LA riots."[31] NBC Nightly News reported that Korean businesses were targeted during the L.A. riots with people in the community complaining that "they keep to themselves, they employ their own, the prices in their stores are too high, their attitude is wrong and they have no respect for black people."[32] Acknowledging the Korean story in Los Angeles will require a more nuanced telling of this chapter in the history of the city.

Ad from Los Angeles City Directory, 1915

The Japanese experience in Los Angeles is another clue. The Japanese owned 120 of 180 produce stalls in the LA city market in 1909.[33] But at the beginning of World War II things changed dramatically. The *LA Times* wrote in 1942 "A viper is nonetheless a viper whenever the egg is hatched--so a Japanese American, born of Japanese parents--grows up to be a Japanese, not an American."[34] In the same year, the board of supervisors for LA county passed a resolution urging the removal of Japanese. The Japanese of the city were taken to Manzanar, the Stables of the Santa Anita Racetrack, other states in the Western United States, and even Canada.

Sadly, this wasn't the first-time Asian immigrants in general, or the Japanese in particular, were treated unjustly. In 1882 the U.S. Congress had passed the Chinese Exclusion Act. This act stopped any further Chinese immigration to America even if that immigration was to reunify families. In 1907 the "Gentleman's Agreement" between Theodore Roosevelt's administration and the Japanese government was signed. The Japanese, asking on behalf of its Korean protectorate, made immigration from Korea illegal. Japanese immigration had already been slowed from Tokyo, who were upset at the treatment of its citizens in America. Restrictions on Filipino immigrants soon followed. In 1924, all of the restrictions were put together in a comprehensive immigration reform act.[36]

A Japanese Bible study group, 19th Century

These narratives of the Asian experience have become, at least in part, integrated into the story of Los Angeles. They are told as a cautionary tale of the abuse of power which can hinder citizens from pursuing their dreams and finding self-fulfillment in their lives. But there is another part of this story which needs to be given voice. It is found among Japanese Christians who have recounted the story of God's redemptive work in the middle of this oppressive evil.

Christianity was introduced more recently to Japan than to Armenia and Persia. The story takes place around the same time as first contact between the Tongva and the Spanish. Francis Xavier (1506-1552) led the first missionaries to Japan. While in Malacca, on the way back to the Moluccas, Xavier heard of the Japanese people. He met a Japanese man named, Yajiro or Anjiro, who had sought refuge on a Portuguese ship to escape punishment for murder. Xavier used the Portuguese trading ships to enter Japan with Yajiro as his interpreter and guide. In Kagoshima, Yajiro's home, members of his family became some of the first Japanese Christians.[36]

Fast forward to Japanese immigrants in Los Angeles during World War II. While experiencing internment, Japanese Christians turned to their Christian faith:

My father and mother converted to Christianity in Japan, and my father studied for and entered the ministry. I . . . think that they came to the United States in 1922...In 1941, we moved to North Hollywood. Our home was a storefront and was barely large enough to contain the beds we slept in...Our church rented space for worship in an American Legion hall. A few hours after the Japanese Imperial Navy attacked our Pacific Fleet at Pearl Harbor, the FBI came and arrested my father as an enemy alien. Two months later, on February 11, 1942, in Ft. Missoula, Montana, the Enemy Alien Hearing Board for the Southern District of California recommended his internment: 'The board feels that whereas the subject is a preacher and it is a hardship to deprive his church of its minister, still that very fact coupled with his membership in the Veteran's Association above referred to, and the fact of his trip to Japan, Korea, and Manchuria in 1940, makes him potentially more dangerous than if he were a farmer, a storekeeper or the like.' I did not discover this judgement until 1995, when I visited the Pacific Southwest Region of the National Archives, almost fifty-four years later. His being a Christian minister threatened the security of the United States. On April 4, 1942, the remainder of our family went by bus under armed guard to the Manzanar Relocation Center. The next day was Easter, which we celebrated outdoors in the early morning at the foot of the mighty Sierra Nevada and its inspiring Mount Williamson. At the same time, the disorder and desolation of concentration-camp existence were beginning to engulf us. We were living parables whose meaning it would take the rest of my life to understand: the reign of God is here, within us, in our midst, for us to enact in our own lives and history, just as Mount Williamson stood

in its majesty alongside our disorder and desolation. God be
with us.[38]

This new narrative should also include the story of the Evergreen Hostel in
the 1940's, where the American Friends Service and the Presbyterian Church
tried to help the Japanese Americans transition back into everyday life. Their
goal was "to provide temporarily a quiet and inexpensive place where those
who return may live during a period of adjustment."[39]

Another clue is the strong Christian faith of Koreans in Los Angeles.
Christianity came even later to the Koreans than to the Japanese. It has also
spread more rapidly among them. It seems that the first Christians to set foot
on Korean soil were members of the Japanese armies under Hideyoshi (d.
1598). A Japanese commanding officer and many of the soldiers had become
Christian by the work of a missionary and his Japanese assistant.[40] However,
there is no record of Koreans becoming Christian during this invasion by
Japan. In 1619 and 1620 a Chinese Christian scholar, Hsu Kuang-Chi,
planned, unsuccessfully, a mission to Korea.[41] Somewhere around 1644
Johann Adam Schall von Bell, a German Jesuit and astronomer was willing to
take a missionary with him to the region, but "in the troubled conditions
accompanying the Manchu conquest, he was unable to find one."[42] Christian
historian, Dr. Kenneth Scott La Tourette writes, "It was not until 1784 that we
hear of a Korean Christian."[43] Astonishingly, almost 29% of South Koreans
are Christian today. The largest church in the world is in the Korean capital of
Seoul (Yoido Full Gospel Church with 480,000 members). Korean
Christianity has a strong missionary emphasis. In 2000 there were an
estimated 10,646 South Korean Protestant missionaries in 156 countries. In
2016 2,473 Korean missionaries were sent to the United States alone by 79
mission organizations.[44] Korean Christianity is surely having an impact on
the City of Angels.

Korean Bible Study groups, early 20th Century

Finally, one other clue emerges from a voice outside of our common narrative. Our world is increasingly impacted by the mixing of cultures through immigration. Terms such as melting pot, salad bowl, or other more recent ideologies of inclusion like multiculturalism and identity politics have been employed but have fallen short of the goal. Many in the West still struggle with guilt over the Western role in the injustices of the past as well as the Western inability to incorporate the narratives of "the other" into "our own." Of particular concern, it seems, is Western culture "overwhelming" non-Western cultures. Though this concern is historically justified, it is outmoded and may be a remnant of the Western hubris this culture is trying to overcome. Sierra Leonian theologian Dr. Jehu Hanciles reminds us that, "contrary to entrenched notions of Western provenance and dominance within the globalization discourse, non-Western initiatives and movements are among the most powerful forces shaping the contemporary world order."[45]

We don't know where these clues will lead in the story of Los Angeles. If Melchizedek is our guide, they will open up new opportunities for the narrative of Los Angeles to grow and develop. For as we trace the impact of his story in the rest of the Bible, it is clear that Melchizedek opened up the Jewish narrative to story development beyond those who controlled it.

Melchizedek re-appears again in Psalm 110. His story has become integrated into the formal transition of power in the Jewish monarchy. The story of Melchizedek helped Israel to iron out the tensions between prophet, priest and king. The monarchy was the late arrival to Israel as a rejection, according to the prophet Samuel, of God as their king (1 Samuel 8:7). The authority of the priesthood was mediated through the tribe of Levi. The function of the priest and prophet in relationship to God and the people had been established. But what about the Israelite King? Psalm 110 provided an answer. This Psalm, attributed to David, is a "royal psalm," used by the court prophet at the coronation of the King in the Temple.[46] In this Psalm, Melchizedek's story is adapted to call the Israelites to submit to their new Priest-King without dislodging the role and authority of the priests or prophets. They are to follow Abraham's example as he submitted to Melchizedek in Genesis 14.

Early Christians made great use of Psalm 110 to make room for their own Priest-King, Jesus Christ. Psalm 110:1 is the most cited Hebrew Testament passage in the New Testament. It helped Christians continue as monotheists while worshipping Jesus. The Psalm was used to call Christians to confess Jesus as Lord without calling into question the glory of God the Father.

In the New Testament book of Hebrews Melchizedek is again cited to iron out the Judeo-Christian story in light of Jesus Christ. Jesus is understood by Christians to be prophet, priest and king. However, Jesus was not born in the priestly class of Levites. Melchizedek is cited as the forerunner of Christ. Jesus' priesthood was not based upon genealogy or the Jewish law. Like the priesthood of Melchizedek, it worked outside of that narrative. His priesthood is a higher priesthood which embodies divine perfection and has no end.[47] Melchizedek opened the way for Christians to develop the Judeo-Christian narrative in which Jesus Christ is the final Lord of history and the center of all human narratives. This development, as will become clear in the final two chapters, has shaped Christianity in a way that it can be helpful to the development of a more inclusive narrative in Los Angeles.

This guidance of Los Angeles by Christianity might strike some as being the exact opposite of what is true. There is a strong belief that the Christian view of history can only continue the exclusivism which has caused such suffering in our world. However, Christ as Lord requires believers to work beyond predominant ideologies. The Christian story begins with the "level playing field" of "all have sinned a fallen short of the glory of God." It then finds complete forgiveness in the death and resurrection of Jesus, a priest in the order of Melchizedek. The gratitude from this forgiveness, when properly understood and deeply experienced, results in a new kind of inclusion. As Miroslav Volf writes:

> though it is true that Christian religious exclusivists make a clear distinction between the saved and the damned, the consistent among them also--and without contradiction-- reject the distinction between moral insiders and moral outsiders. The Golden Rule, a succinct summary of all Christian moral obligation, commands: 'In everything, do to others as you would have them to do you'--do to all others, not just to a select few.[48]

This peculiarly Christian form of exclusivity empowers the faith to transcend national and ideological histories. As Richard Bauckham puts it, "Worship...is the source of resistance to the idolatries of the public world."[49]

Los Angeles needs to find a way to open dialogue between the common narrative of the city and the narrative of Angelenos from the non-Western world. Christianity can help. In this open dialogue the 'other' is free to share their story in a way that allows the expectations and intentions of the mainstream narrative to be resisted. As Alistair McFadyen put it in *A Call to Personhood*, "There is a readiness to allow the calls of others to transform us in response." For, as Jehu Hanciles writes, "the meaningful long-term solution to the current crisis will remain elusive without some adaptive compromise . . . that involves cultural accommodation and a willingness to form new collective identities."[50] By engaging the diverse narratives of Angelenos, Los Angeles can continue to provide inspiring possibilities for the future, not only in this city, but in other cities as well.

Lovejoy

Chapter 8

The Sign of Jonah in City of Angels

What would we really feel if we were suddenly catapulted into... [a] story-world where we are not necessarily at the center of the world? -Yvonne Sherwood[1]

The life of William Seymour is a quintessential L.A. story; a dream pursued and a dream found wanting. For most Angelenos, he lived and died on the margins of the city. But Seymour's life in Los Angeles can be judged by different measure; a measure of success integral to his Judeo-Christian faith. Such a measure opens up new possibilities, not only for the story of his life, but for the story of life in La La Land. For William Seymour's life can be read as a "sign of Jonah" for the City of Angels.

William Joseph Seymour had a dream. It was quite a dream for the son of former slaves. Born in south Louisiana in 1870, Seymour had a dream that, as he described it, "Our colored brethren must love our white brethren and respect them in truth so that the word of God can have its free course, and our white brethren must love their colored brethren and respect them in truth so that the Holy Spirit won't be grieved."[2] This dream formed before Seymour arrived in Los Angeles. In 1900, in Cincinnati, Seymour responded to a deep spiritual experience by joining the "Evening Light Saints."[3] Their leader, Daniel Warner, emphasized the importance of Christian unity across racial boundaries.[4] A few years later in Houston, Texas, Seymour's dream developed further under the tutelage of Charles Parham, a man who had experienced "baptism indicated by tongues" at the Topeka outpouring.[5] Seymour had to listen to Parham's teachings from the other side of the door due to the Jim

145

Crow laws in effect in Texas at the time. Parham called him the humblest man that he had ever met.

Seymour received an offer to lead a congregation in Los Angeles. Parham stood against it arguing that he was not yet ready for such a position. But in 1906, Seymour left to pursue his dream in Los Angeles understanding his ministry to be part of the "Restoration Faith Movement," a group which, in his words, "stands for the restoration of faith once delivered to the saints--the old-time religion, camp meetings, revivals, missions, street and prison work, and Christian unity everywhere." He continued, "We are not fighting men or churches but seeking to displace dead forms and creeds and wild fanaticism with living, practical Christianity. 'Love, faith, unity' is our watchword."[6]

As with so many before him, the pursuit of his dream in Los Angeles didn't come easily. In 1906, soon after his arrival, he was locked out of the church by Julia Hutchinson, the leader of the church who had offered him the position that brought him to the city. Five years later Seymour himself would padlock the church to shut out another preacher, William Durham, who had attempted to take over leadership of the congregation while Seymour was out of state. Between these two events, however, Seymour's dream "took on flesh" in what is now known as the Azusa Street Revival.

Seymour was discouraged when he was locked out of the church. His premillennialist[7] views as well as his understanding of the gift of tongues were contrary to Hutchinson's beliefs. So, just days after his arrival in L.A., he was unemployed. Seymour decided to fast and pray. Edward S. Lee, of the Peniel Mission in Los Angeles, joined him. Word began to spread. Others joined them. The group increased their prayer from 5 to 7 hours a day.

The group grew in numbers and moved to a larger space, a house on Bonnie Brae Street. During one meeting there, Seymour spoke on Acts 2:4.[8] The congregation began speaking in tongues. This experience caused the gatherings to grow even more. They moved again to accommodate the growing group. Their new location was 312 Azusa Street, a former site of the 1st A.M.E. church.[9] This became the main location of the Azusa Revival.

312 Azuza Street

Historians of the Azusa Street Revival date the event from 1906 to 1909. Dr. Cecil Robeck describes it in this way, "The revival came to an African-American congregation whose pastor had a vision for multiracial and multiethnic worship, which led to salvation, sanctification, and baptism in the Holy Spirit."[10] *The Apostolic Faith* newsletter, developed by Seymour and Ms. Clara Lum, spread the news of the revival well beyond Los Angeles, even having an impact in other parts of the United States and the world.[11]

Azuza Street Leadership

In 1908, however, Seymour's dream took an L.A. turn. Clara Lum took the national and international supporter list and moved to the Northwest to start a new ministry with Florence Crawford. They continued to produce

The Apostolic Faith newsletter with this list but without any mention of the Los Angeles ministry. The newsletter began to solicit donations for the new ministry. Seymour travelled north to try to heal the growing divide, to no avail. Then Seymour's local ministry started to split along racial lines. On October 2, 1922, a group of 200 mostly African-Americans gathered for Seymour's funeral.[12]

After his burial, Seymour's wife, Jenny, took his mantle as the leader of the Apostolic Faith Mission for the next 8 years. The fellowship numbered about 40. In 1930, a stranger asked to join their prayers. Rutherford D. Griffith was an 87-year-old Anglo man who claimed to be a missionary to Africa and the previous pastor of a number of African-American congregations.[13] Griffith impressed the multiethnic congregation, especially the whites. He became a regular part of the congregation's worship services. Finally, he approached Jenny Seymour telling her he had the support of the congregation and the church was now his.

Griffith pushed the issue. On June 16, 1931, the LAPD locked the doors of the church to enforce a pause on the dispute until the court could make a decision. They eventually ruled in Jenny's favor. But by then the church had dwindled to 27 people. They had to take on additional debt to keep up with the mortgage. Late that year the city condemned the building as a fire hazard and demolished it. In 1933 the mortgage on the property was signed over to the city. Jenny continued to lead the remnant of the congregation in her home on Bonnie Brae Street until her health deteriorated. She died on July 2, 1936 and was buried next to her husband.

If only Seymour had been able to break through the racial divisions and power plays that beset his ministry. If only he had been able to build a sustainable church on Azusa Street. If only his life ended with a "ride into the sunset." Then he could be our hero. Such stories make inspiring Hollywood movies. But, as we have seen, they are pure fiction when it comes to the history of Los Angeles. Instead, William Seymour's life, like Henry Jensen and G.J.

Griffith in chapter 2, are stories of human powerlessness, of vulnerability and frustration, of incomplete dreams both in life and in death. Even at the apex of Seymour's ministry in L.A., when the Azusa Revival was gaining strength, the city saw it as something to ridicule. The *Los Angeles Daily Times* published an article on April 18, 1906, entitled, "Weird Babel of Tongues: New Sect of Fanatics is Breaking Loose." The paper described the momentary fulfillment of Seymour's dream in the following way: "Colored people and a sprinkling of whites compose the congregation, and night is made hideous in the neighborhood by the howling of worshippers who spend hours swaying forth and back in a nerve-racking attitude of prayer and supplication." Seymour's life, like so many lives in L.A., is a story of broken dreams teaching lessons of futility. If this "L.A. turn" eventually consumes everyone who pursues their dream in Los Angeles, we might ask, why even try?

This struggle with fatalism has always been a part of being human. It surfaces when we hit our limitations. As modern and post-modern people we lack the resources to make sense of such situations. But in the ancient world there was a method of storytelling which helped people find meaning in their limitations. These stories embraced the reality of human powerlessness,

vulnerability and frustration in a way that opened up new possibilities for the future. The book of Jonah in the Hebrew Testament of the Bible is one of the better known examples of this kind of storytelling. It can be helpful to us as we struggle with the L.A. turn.

Most people think of the story of Jonah as little more than a story about a man swallowed by a whale. A literal interpretation of this story has become part of the tug-of-war between theists and atheists in the public square. On the one hand, according to some, you must believe that Jonah survived three days in the belly of a very large fish if you are a faithful Christian. On the other, you cannot believe in this religious "fish story" if you have any intelligence. These interpretations, however, tell us more about our own cultural issues than they do about the message of Jonah. For this little book holds a thematic quality which is strange to modern and post-modern ears but is potentially powerful for the City of Angels.

Jonah is unusual, even in the Bible. For Jonah is a prophet of Israel. The book that bears his name is quite unlike books bearing the names of other prophets like Isaiah, Ezekiel, and Malachi. For one thing, it is the only prophetic book that doesn't focus on the substance of the prophet's preaching. Instead, the book focuses on Jonah's journey. It takes place in 4 parts: his initial flight from God's call (1:1-16), his three days in the belly of the fish (1:17-2:10), his ministry in Nineveh (3), and his petulant response to God's mercy extended to the Ninevites (4). A prophet like Jeremiah represents God over and above nationalist priorities. But from the beginning of this prophetic book, Jonah embodies the national and religious ethnocentrism which sees God as the exclusive property of the Israelites. The tension of the story is not between God and his people, but between God and his prophet. Jonah sees God as the exclusive possession of the Israelites and acts accordingly. As such, Jonah is an anti-hero who works counter to the arc of the story. Contrary to Jonah's intentions, the story moves relentlessly forward to establish God's mercy beyond national boundaries.[14] Jonah, God's prophet, is the one who needs to repent.

This ancient and very Christian story contrasts sharply with the Western democratic vision of life. We have been taught to see history as the ultimate scene of human destiny. We cheer courageous people who overcome the barriers set up against them to achieve their freely chosen goals. We "boo" those who use their power and wealth to stop individuals from achieving their dream. Such stories inspire us to break through barriers to become the people we want to be.

The weakness of such stories is that they are unable to find any meaning in what we have been calling the L.A. turn. A life like William Seymour's can only be seen as a failure. Jonah helps us break through to a new interpretation of Seymour's life and to the theme of the L.A. turn.

Jonah confuses our expectations. He is not the gritty and determined hero who drives the narrative with his pursuit of self-fulfillment. Instead, his role is to make the *wrong* decisions in a narrative which reveals the narrowness of his point of view. His three days and three nights in the whale show his inability to drive the narrative. He is being taken where he doesn't want to go, by a means he is powerless to stop, for a purpose in conflict with his own self-interest. This role continues right up to the end of the story. As Gerhard von Rad puts it:

> The ridiculous, stubborn Jonah, grudging God's mercy to the heathen, but filled with joy at the shade of the castor oil plant, and then wanting to die when he sees it withering away, is unable to impede God's saving thoughts--they achieve their goal in spite of everything.[15]

What if we look at Seymour's life in Los Angeles with this type of storytelling in mind? Not that Seymour was disobeying God as Jonah did. But Seymour was playing a similar role in the story of the Azusa Street Revival as Jonah did in his story. Now Seymour doesn't have to carry the plot of the story. That is not his purpose. His role instead is to be the vulnerable (humble) man who doesn't drive the narrative. The inconsistencies and frustrations of the story become a sign that his life is being driven by a story of grace and mercy far greater than he is.

From this perspective we are encouraged to search Seymour's life for a story that is bigger than he is. Here we discover a story that is truly global in scope. The theme of speaking in tongues, for example, played a key role in Seymour's revival. But speaking in tongues began long before Seymour's life and continued long after it ended. It is an experience which is well represented in the ancient world and is found in a number of tribal religions. It has been a part of Christianity since its beginning.[16] This religious experience seems to have made its first appearance in the modern era in 17th century France when Isabella Vincent spoke in tongues.[17] In the 1830's glossolalia, another term to describe speaking in tongues, was experienced by English Quakers and by the Catholic Apostolic Church in the United States. After the Civil War speaking in tongues spread through congregations affiliated with the Holiness Movement led by Rev. R. B. Swan in Rhode Island. As he once wrote, "In the year 1875 our Lord began to pour out upon us His Spirit: my wife and I with a few others began to utter a few words in the 'unknown tongue.'"[18] This experience of "fire baptism" as it was then called, became the Fire Baptized Holiness Association which, broadly, set the state for Seymour's ministry.[19]

Seymour's experience with revival also has a much larger arc in human history. The Azusa Street Revival was the result of a preparation that takes us back in time and place to 1904 in Wales. Evan Robert was a 26-year-old minister in training who had once been a coal miner. He claimed direct visions from the Holy Spirit and developed, as others have testified, an increased ability to follow the lead of the Holy Spirit. His ministry resulted in a revival which lasted less than a year but saw the conversion of 100,000 people. This revival had a lasting impact in Wales. The churches in Wales were full for the next twenty years.[20] Even the mules in Wales had to be retrained. The converted teamsters no longer urged them on with anger and cursing. New ways to motivate the mules had to be found.

Joseph Smale, pastor of First Baptist Church, Los Angeles, wanted to go deeper in his faith. Having heard of the events of the Welsh revival, he travelled there to meet with Robert in 1904. Upon his return to Los Angeles, Smale was instrumental in a 4-month revival in the city. He opened his church for intercessory prayer meetings which drew people from across Los Angeles. A key theme to their prayers was for a new Pentecost.[21] They saw their movement as only the beginning. As Smale summarized it, "Pentecost, not *come*, but *is coming*."

Smale lost his pastorate. Some of the leaders of First Baptist opposed the spontaneity of the prayer times and forced him to resign. Undeterred, he formed The New Testament Church of Los Angeles where the prayers continued. In 1905 he preached a series of sermons entitled, "The Pentecostal Blessing,"[22] which many see as preparing Los Angeles for Seymour's ministry.

It was at about this time that Julia Hutchinson began teaching sanctification as a dramatic personal experience subsequent to salvation. A group began to grow around her teaching in the Second Baptist Church of L.A., but the pastor asked her to leave.[23] The small group of nine primarily African-American families that had formed around her ministry joined a tent meeting. Later they established a Holiness Mission on Santa Fe Street[24] before Hutchinson sent her invitation to Elder William J. Seymour to become their pastor.

Looking at Seymour's life from this perspective, we can include the impact of his ministry after his own death as a critical part of the story of his life. Alfred Goodrich Garr, Sr (1874-1944), for example, was the pastor of Burning Bush Mission in Los Angeles. In 1906 he participated in Seymour's Azusa Street Mission where some say he was the first Caucasian pastor in this revival to receive baptism in the Holy Spirit with speaking in tongues. The experience changed his family's life. "Convinced that some of the tongues were real languages, given for the purpose of mission, the Garrs participated in the strong thrust of the early Pentecostal movement into foreign missions."[25] Seeing their experience as a continuation of the story in Acts 2, Garr believed that he had been given an Indian language and his wife Tibetan and Chinese. They went to India in 1907 but were disappointed to find out that they did not have the supernatural linguistic skills they thought they had. However, they ministered by preaching the new Pentecostal doctrines at an American Board of Commissioners for Foreign Missions church. Until they were evicted. But they had had their impact. A deacon of that church, Mok Lai Chi, became the driving force behind the Pentecostal community in Hong Kong.[26] This is only one of many stories that can be told to illustrate the global impact of Seymour's life.

Missionaries from the revival went to 50 countries to spread the ministry. Wonderfully, Julia Hutchinson, who had locked the church doors on Seymour, was impacted by the revival and became a missionary to Africa. Another woman, Mary Ramsey, attended the Azusa Street meetings in Los Angeles in 1907. She then went as a missionary to Korea, eventually starting a Bible school. One of the students in her first class was David Yongii Cho. He would become the founding pastor of the Yoido Full Gospel Church, the world's largest Christian congregation in the 20th century, with a membership of 830,000. It is not an overstatement to say, "Azusa Street played a major role in the development of modern Pentecostalism--a Movement that changed the religious landscape and became the most vibrant force for world evangelization in the 20th century."[27]

Today, more than a century after Seymour died, scholars from many different Christian traditions acknowledge the importance of the Pentecostal Movement, growing from the Azusa Street Revival, to the history of Christianity. Anglican John Taylor tells us, "The membership of the Pentecostal churches, which has stemmed mainly from the Topeka and Los Angeles revival in the USA at the beginning of this century, still vastly outnumbers those in the traditional churches."[28]

And yet, these stories are not well known. This is true of the stories in the Bible as well. The Biblical story is almost always written from the fringes of the global history which surrounds it. The Bible certainly recognizes dominant narratives of the Babylonians, the Persians, and Romans. But these narratives are simply the backdrop for the story of the people of God. Rather than giving prominence to these dominant stories, the Bible asserts the transcendent power of God over these oppressive narratives. Thus, in the Bible the human heroes do not have to win to be "successful." It is often when the human protagonist fails that the Biblical narratives shine most brightly.

Take Jesus, for example. He is the main character of the Gospels. He is, as his Romans executioner Pontius Pilate put it, the "King of the Jews." We read of Jesus' growing popularity among the masses of people as he teaches and heals. He demonstrates wisdom and cleverness as he thwarts growing attempts to derail his ministry. But his life in all four of the Gospels takes an "L.A. turn." He ends up in the Garden of Gethsemane waiting to be arrested

155

and crucified. As he faces his death he prays, 'Father, if you are willing, take this cup from me; yet not my will, but yours be done.'(Luke 22:42) The Gospels tell the story of a "hero" who is unable to stop his crucifixion, who spends three days and nights in a tomb he did not want to be in, who lives and dies for a purpose beyond his self-interest.

At the time of his crucifixion, Jesus' life and ministry was a failure in any human sense of the word. He had no published works, no conferences inviting him to speak, no movement of thousands obeying his every word. Only twelve disciples, one of whom betrayed him into the hands of his enemies and eleven others who scattered at the news of his impending death. He was unjustly crucified, as Douglas Adams of *Hitchhiker's Guide to the Galaxy* succinctly describes it, "for saying how great it would be to be nice to people for a change."[29] But, like Jonah, his "failed" life would play an important role in the larger story.

Jesus himself connects his life with Jonah. In the Gospel of Matthew he tells a riddle which he calls "the sign of the prophet Jonah." He is in the middle of a very tense interaction with religious leaders who oppose him. After Jesus heals a demon-possessed man, the Pharisees and Sadducees accuse him of being motivated by Satan. Jesus points out the flaw in their argument by telling them that a Kingdom divided against itself cannot stand. They then shift their attack on him, asking him for a sign to prove to them that he is from God. Jesus cleverly responds with his riddle. "For as Jonah was three days and three nights in the belly of a huge fish, so the Son of Man will be three days and three nights in the heart of the earth" (Matthew 12:40). He is giving them fair warning that he, like Jonah, will succeed by failing.

Seymour, like Jesus, is a sign of Jonah. Jonah's story was a morality tale for the people of Israel, reminding them of how easily they could find themselves working against God's purposes, against the master theme of the story God is writing in human history. With tongue firmly planted in cheek the author of the book of Jonah makes the critical point that God's purposes of mercy and forgiveness are not thwarted by our ideological battle lines. We, like the prophet Jonah, become a foil for God's mercy--a mercy that continues unabated beyond all of our attempts to contain and control it. Seymour's life, in its vulnerability and humility, makes a similar point for Los Angeles.

Seymour, like Jesus, ran toward God's calling rather than away from it. But as in the story of Jonah, the mercy of God extended well beyond anything he did. His life in Los Angeles, as Jonah's story in Nineveh, reminds us that God's mercy pushes well beyond anything we do to try to control history. The story God is writing is much greater than anything that the L.A. turn can throw at us. As a matter of fact, the story God is writing can redeem even the worst Los Angeles turn. Because the real story line of human existence is the forgiveness and mercy of God.

The sign of Jonah makes it clear that the witness of Christianity in Los Angeles cannot be that faith in Jesus somehow guarantees the fulfillment of dreams in a way that Los Angeles cannot. Christianity cannot erase the L.A. turn. Instead, it calls us to share in the suffering of the city. It calls us to respond in forgiveness and mercy, in a way that points to the story that God is writing. This story transcends all human stories in every city on the planet. As a Medieval Jewish homily tells us, in an added conclusion of the story of Jonah, "At that very moment, [Jonah] fell flat on his face saying, 'Direct the world according to the attribute of mercy, as it is written, 'Mercy and forgiveness belong to the Lord.'"[30]

If we extend the sign of Jonah to other stories of the L.A. turn, we find the way opened to this theme that is so desperately missing from post-modern civil discourse. Forgiveness and mercy are writ large in the life of Jonah, in the life of Jesus, and in the life of William Seymour. We are all vulnerable to the curse of the L.A. turn. We all need forgiveness and mercy. For some, accepting human vulnerability seems to betray our pursuit of justice. But the failure to embrace human vulnerability was what caused Jonah to miss the point of his story. Responding to human vulnerability with mercy and forgiveness, not only among our friends, but also among our enemies, does not impede justice, it only delegitimizes revenge. This is the message at the heart of the story of Jonah. Rabbi Ed Feinstein, Senior Rabbi of Valley Beth Shalom in the city of Encino, California, aptly summarizes Jonah as follows,

> Then, one day, God appeared to Jonah and shattered his world. In God there is a unity beneath the divisions, wholeness behind disjunction: you and me, us and them, ours and theirs. Though separated on the surface, we are deeply connected within. The boundaries of self, God insists, must include the other.[31]

If Angelenos can accept the sign of Jonah and come together with forgiveness and mercy, Seymour's dream might still come true in the City of Angles:

> Our colored brethren must love our white brethren and respect them in truth so that the word of God can have its free course, and our white brethren must love their colored brethren and respect them in truth so that they Holy Spirit won't be grieved. I hope we won't have any more trouble and division of spirit.[32]

Chapter 9

The Future City

And he carried me away in the Spirit to a mountain great and high, and showed me the Holy City, Jerusalem, coming down out of heaven from God. It shone with the glory of God, and its brilliance was like that of a very precious jewel, like a jasper, clear as crystal. -Revelation. 21:10-11

The Rialto Theatre is an iconic Los Angeles landmark. The 1,200-seat theater built in 1925 is a symbol of the "glory days" of the entertainment industry in this city. It has been the scene of Vaudeville acts, of trapeze artists and, more recently, a decade long run of the Rocky Horror Picture Show. But in 1968 it was the scene of a fire. In 1977 the owner had plans to raze the building and make it into a parking lot. In 2007 it was named a landmark only to be closed to the public in 2010 because part of the facade fell onto the sidewalk. In 2016 its iconic role was revived by the movie, *LaLa Land*. Today, there continues to be a gap between the dream of the Theatre and its present reality.

In 2017, the pastor of a Christian congregation in Los Angeles announced a new, 20-year lease of the Rialto. The church plans to restore the building while developing a new satellite congregation in South Pasadena, where the Theatre is located. After a multimillion-dollar renovation, and at the end of their lease, they will give it back as a gift to L.A. Such a vision embodies the role that Christians can play in the future of the city.

Christians have an important role to play in the future of the City of Angels. To understand this role, we must go back to the beginning of the Christian story. The book of Genesis begins with a sense of anticipation. There is darkness and emptiness. But the Spirit is hovering over the waters. Something is about to happen. With the call, "Let there be light!" the Universe begins. This creative act continues with the planet earth taking shape. Then plants, and animals and humans (Genesis 1). As the Biblical story continues cities form. Gatherings of human beings like the city of Los Angeles.

The Bible also speaks of the end of the human story. As the Bible begins with anticipation, it ends with expectation. The author of Revelation sees another act of creation in the future. This new creation is a city. This city fulfills all human aspiration. But it is not a city built by human hands. It is a city which comes down from heaven, ready for human habitation (Revelation 22). We inhabit the time between creation and the arrival of this "New Jerusalem."

Western culture has "marinated" in this biblical view of the beginning and the end for generations. It has flavored our whole perception of time. Lesslie Newbigin reminds us that "From the time of Augustine and Orosius up to the enlightenment in the eighteenth century, world history was on the basis of that vision of history which is embodied in the Bible."[1] Historian Karl Lowith agrees: "It is only because of our habit of thinking in terms of Christian tradition that the formal division of all historical time into past, present, and future times seems so entirely natural and self-evident."[2]

Modern Western culture has been working to remove this Christian influence. Enlightenment thinkers, like Auguste Comte, Pierre-Joseph Proudhon, and Karl Marx, rejected the idea of divine providence and replaced it with a belief in human progress. Their efforts have largely succeeded. Western scholarship regularly rejects the Christian view of history as scientifically naive. Many hold it responsible for the failings of Western culture: oppression, injustice, environmental degradation. However, this rejection has not gotten to the roots of Christian influence on Western history. Modern consciousness continues to hold deep assumptions based upon Christian theology. Assumptions such as past, present and future.

These Christian concepts, however, have been distorted. The human being has become "the bearer of the meaning of his own history."[3] The burden of history is completely our responsibility. The experiences of anticipation and expectation are lost. The past is the source of our present problems, brought on by the inadequacies of the generations that have come before us. The future will only be bright if we make it that way. Given all of the struggles of the present, brought on by all of the injustices of the past, a dark future is the most likely outcome. There is no riding into the sunset. The future will not be a "brilliant city" but a dystopian nightmare.

Perhaps one of the most well-regarded dystopian films is the movie *Blade Runner*. This "Raymond Chandler meets science fiction" story was originally set in San Francisco as a book, entitled, *Do Androids Dream of Electric Sheep?* The movie version was moved to Los Angeles in a dark, strangely rainy and not so strangely crowded future city. It features a number of historical city landmarks. Harrison Ford plays Deckard, a retired Los

Angeles police officer who is caught in a battle between androids and their human makers. The Ennis Brown House forms the backdrop for his apartment. The dark path between his home and the precinct where he works is the Second Street Tunnel between Figueroa and Hill. Another character, Sebastian, is an android maker who lives in what was once the Pan Am building on South Broadway, across from the Yukon Hotel. This dystopian city of Los Angeles is the back drop for expressions of some of the deepest longings of the human heart.

We are attracted to dystopian views of the future. So many of our stories of the future, *Blade Runner*, *Mad Max,* and *Zombie Apocalypse*, express the frustration of our hopes and dreams. We fear that our efforts to overcome our own limitations will fail. And, given our view of history, such failure means there is no hope for the future. Hollywood stories of this genre are often morality plays which reinforce the idea that without progress the future will be catastrophic. Their moral is that "the good" requires our continued vigilance. If we don't stand against those who promote "regression" they will walk us into an oppressive and even apocalyptic future. These people must be excluded for the sake of our civilization. This is a dangerous approach which produce the results that we set out to prevent. "As Friedrich Nietzsche and the neo-Nietzscheans (such as Michel Foucalt) have pointed out, exclusion is often the evil perpetrated by '*the good*' and barbarity produced by *civilization*."4

Post-modern thinking urges us to reject this secular view of history. Jean-Francoise Lyotard, for example, in *La Condition Postmoderne*, warns against the dangers of this idea of progress. Christianity agrees with this post-modern critique. The popular imagination regularly confuses the post-modern rejection of the secular view of progress as a rejection of Christianity. But these philosophers are rejecting the view of history which developed form the partial rejection the Christian view of history. The words of one of the most important American theologians of the 20th century seem relevant here: "The evil habit of men (sic) in all times to criticize their predecessors for having seen only half the truth, hides from them their own partiality and incompleteness."[5]

In 1892, the same year that Edward Doheny first found oil in Los Angeles, Johannes Weiss wrote a scholarly tome which reminded Western theologians that the coming of God's kingdom as proclaimed by Jesus Christ, was not the result of human action, but from God alone.[6] The future city comes, is not built up from the ground by human hands, but descends from heaven by the hand of God.

Christian history begins with anticipation. It ends with expectation. At its center is the experience of wonder. Christianity understands the life, death, and resurrection of Jesus Christ as being the center of human history. All time from the creation to the birth of Jesus became BC or "before Christ." Human history from Christ's birth to the coming of the Kingdom of God is AD, or "in the year of our Lord." From the Christian point of view, the child of a working class Israeli family from a back-water town called Nazareth, who was conceived out of wedlock and born in a manger is the arc of all of human history. Wonder, awe, and surprise indeed!

This understanding of the center of history further defines the time in which we live. Jesus came proclaiming that the Kingdom of God had come near (Mark 1:14-15). Through faith in the resurrected Christ, his followers experienced a foretaste of the future city in the present. The Apostle Paul, for example, wrote, "And you also were included in Christ when you heard the message of truth, the gospel of salvation. When you believed, you were marked in him with a seal, the promised Holy Spirit, who is a deposit guaranteeing our inheritance until the redemption of those who are God's possession--to the praise of his glory" (Ephesians 1:13-15).   But that experience is limited in the present. Some Christian scholars refer to the present as "now and not yet." We experience the nearness of the kingdom now, but the future city is not yet here in its fullness.

Living in the now and the not yet means that life is a series of events which only become meaningful in relation to the city which is coming. This is not fatalistic. The sovereign God is directing human history in a way which is faithful to the biblical story. God is utterly free in the way in which this story will be fulfilled.[7] The anticipation, expectation and wonder of this view of human life motivates creative and loving responses to the frustrations of life which inevitably come our way. These creative acts of love on behalf of the city are, as Albert Schweitzer once called them, "acted prayers" for the coming of the future city.[8] As Karl Barth has written: "He that gazes upon this earthly fragment of the world, and perceives in the life of Jesus, and beyond it, the redemption which shall come; he it is that hears the creative Voice of God."[9]

This understanding of human life is expressed in the history of Christianity. Rather than being a progressive extension from Jerusalem to the rest of the world, Christianity is serial in nature. Dr. Walls sketched this serial nature of Christianity in his 1982 Finlayson Lecture in Edinburgh. The first age is the Jewish age, the initial phase of Christianity as a sect of the Jewish faith formed around a distinct interpretation of the Jewish Messiah. The second age is, according to Walls, the "Hellenistic-Roman" period in which the church became predominantly Gentile. During this age, the idea of orthodoxy, with its emphasis on a series of propositional truths arrived at by logical argument, was deeply impressed on the Christian faith. The third "Barbarian age" was the time when Christianity found new life in an unexpected place, among the very barbarians who overthrew the Roman empire. It is only in the fourth phase of Walls' schema that we come to the church we have been discussing in our story of Los Angeles. Three times before Christianity came to Los Angeles, it has become centered in one cultural location in the world and spread outwards before that center declines. This movement is peculiar to Christianity, making itself at home for a time in a particular culture and then moving to a new center.[10] We have seen Christianity's local adaptations in Los Angeles. It made its home in Spanish colonial culture but failed to find a lasting place in Native American culture. It pulled back to embrace life in the Mexican Rancho. Then it grew dramatically in its Protestant expression with help from the already converted Mid-Westerners who made the City of Angels their home. Today it is in yet another period of transition.

As we have seen in the story of Los Angeles, Christians have had difficulty making these transitions. Each impress of Christianity, in a particular geographical and culture center, becomes inseparable from that generation's expression of the faith. Letting go of the institutional forms that have supported the established expression of Christianity feels, to those particular Christians, like a betrayal of the faith itself.

Christianity has had to develop methods to help followers think outside of what they know so they might follow God into a new expression of the faith. The "New Jerusalem" in the biblical book of Revelation is a very early example of this. This vision, contrary to Marxist critique, is not an escape from reality. As Dr. Richard Bauckham says in his commentary on the book, "part of the strategy of Revelation, in creating a symbolic world for its readers to enter, was to redirect their imaginative response to the world."[11] The tension between the dream of the coming city and the present day reality motivated adaptation and creativity.

> And he carried me away in the Spirit to a mountain great and high,
> and showed me the Holy City, Jerusalem, coming down out of heaven
> from God. It shone with the glory of God, and its brilliance was like
> that of a very precious jewel, like a jasper, clear as crystal. -Revelation
> 21:10-11

This vision of the "New Jerusalem" opened up the possibility of creative adaptation in early Christianity, which was deeply rooted in the earthly Jerusalem. It did so by creating tension between the Jerusalem of the present and the "New Jerusalem" of the future. "Christianity came into being by dislocating Jerusalem, the sacred city of its parents' Hebrew faith . . . The old Jerusalem became the New Jerusalem 'above' whose citizens were to be the whole realm of redeemed humanity."[12] The New Jerusalem "represents the true fulfillment of the ideal city, a city truly worth belonging to."[13]

The vision of the "New Jerusalem" can help Angelenos adapt to their future as well. Los Angeles is a city stuck in the ideological crises of liberal Western democracy. It is living off the fumes of ideas from days gone by. A new vision is needed, a "New Los Angeles." Christianity in Los Angeles is also stuck in the past. Much of Christianity's time, energy and resources in Los Angeles is spent upholding institutional structures that are no longer working. A renewed vision of the "New Jerusalem" is needed so that they might "be open to that experience of God which first launched Christianity and to let that experience . . . create new expressions of faith, worship and mission at both the individual and corporate level."[14]

If Christianity in L.A. can embrace this openness to God and re-engage its ability to create new expressions of the faith, Christianity in the City of Angels can engage in adaptive experiments in Christian ministry. These experiments not only will help Christianity to be planted and to grow in the next generation, but will also help Angelenos to heal the deep wounds of dreams unfulfilled and unfulfilling.

166

One night, Anthony Kiedis, of the band, The Red Hot Chili Peppers, walked to the bridge near MacArthur park in Los Angeles to buy drugs. He was lamenting the loss of relationship with Ione Skye, a woman from New York whose mother was Jewish and whose father was from Britain. Since Kiedis's break up with her, Ione Skye had married another man in a Hindu ceremony. That night, the pain of the break up as well as the distance he was feeling from his bandmates, left him thinking about the city of Los Angeles. L.A. seemed to be his only companion. Kiedis wrote:

> I felt an unspoken bond between me and my city. I'd spent so much time wandering through the streets of L.A. and hiking through the Hollywood Hills that I sensed there was a nonhuman entity, maybe the spirit of the hills and the city, who had me in her sights and was looking after me.[15]

He put this experience to music in a song entitled, "Under the Bridge."

> Sometimes I feel like I don't have a partner
> Sometimes I feel like my only friend
> Is the city I live in, the city of angels
> Lonely as I am, together we cry.
>
> I drive on the streets cause she's my companion
> I walk through her hills cause she knows who I am
> She sees my good deeds . . .
>
> It's hard to believe that there's nobody out there
> It's hard to believe that I'm all alone
> At least I have her love, the city, she loves me
> Lonely as I am, together we cry"[16]

In an interesting contrast to "California Dreamin," Kiedis doesn't seek to escape the city he calls home. Instead, he finds comfort in Los Angeles. Many people in Los Angeles, like Kiedis are on a spiritual journey. But few look to the institutional church for spiritual guidance. How might someone like Kiedis make a fruitful connection between his journey and Christianity? How might be find the expectation, anticipation, and wonder that flows out of a creative tension between this city and the future city? This is the adaptive challenge for Christianity in the City of Angels.

If Christianity is going to rise to this challenge, it will happen through people like Cat Moore. Cat graduated summa cum laude with honors in philosophy from the University of Southern California in 2005. Before and after that time (from 2001-2011) she was an apprentice in applied theology under Dr. Dallas Willard. She has developed a ministry whose creativity and adaptive ability move far outside of the imagination of institutional Christianity. Dr. Willard spoke of her as one of the students who gave him hope for the future of the church.

I had the opportunity to talk with Cat one afternoon about her ministry. She told me of the many friendships she had developed in the community of Atwater Village in Los Angeles, focusing particularly on her relationship with Sandra.

Cat had met Sandra in an Atwater Starbucks about seven years before our conversation. Cat lived in neighborhood and this was part of her regular routine; to pick up a chai before going on a stroller walk in the neighborhood surrounding the cafe with her baby son, Noah. On this particular day, Sandra came up to Cat and Noah wanting to touch Noah's tiny feet. Letting a stranger touch her son was a stretch for Cat. She reluctantly agreed. "He's sleeping so be careful," she said. This was enough to start the relationship.

The relationship continued with Cat and Sandra exchanging greetings when their paths crossed at Starbucks. Cat noticed that Sandra dressed like the stereotypical bohemian. She seemed very intense and a bit abrasive.

About five and a half years later Cat started going to a restaurant in the community with more space than Starbucks in order to build relationships and organize meetings with more people in the neighborhood. She noticed that Sandra also frequented the restaurant, getting meals between work. They began to eat some meals together in this new restaurant. They had more time to go deeper with each other than talking over a cup of coffee would allow.

It was during these discussions that Sandra told Cat that she was a crystal healer and channeler. She owned a crystal wholesale company. She made sales all over the country. She believed in past lives and that, at some point, she herself had been a crystal. In her present life she channels one specific spirit named "Terrance." She considers him an unseen friend who brings information from the spiritual realm that she can share with the people that she is caring for. This was all new for Cat. She asked Sandra all kinds of follow up questions about her life. Her past has been challenging, including struggles with addiction.

Sandra was an amazing listener. As Cat continued having conversations with Sandra she found that, in many ways, Sandra was an authority on emotional and spiritual health. Her responses to things that Cat shared with her showed wisdom and insight. Sandra was willing to "be there" for Cat at any time. Cat's friendship with Sandra became one of the most surprising friendships Cat has ever had. Sandra was equally surprised at what had developed between them. She told Cat that she never thought she would be friends with a Christian. She shared that the relationship had helped her to have a safe place to do some healing, to expand her own mind, and to move forward on her journey of surrendering and loving.

Cat and Sandra

"What did you have to 'unlearn' to join God in this ministry?", I asked. Cat quickly responded, "Everything!" Then after thinking a bit longer she said, "Gosh, where do I even begin? I think I had so limited God . . . and I didn't even know that I had. I found this out when things exploded in my life and I couldn't use the tools and frameworks I was used to using. My intellectual and spiritual habits soured through spiritual abuse and triggered trauma for me. I had to relearn that these weren't the only tools to engage and be reached by God. He showed me a new way experientially that quite literally blew my mind-in a good way!"

She spoke of God's "wildness" in working through people who weren't Christian. She experienced God working through children's literature she read with her son. She felt God speak to her through the beauty of nature on her walks. She realized ministry wasn't about her categories and competencies. It often wasn't even about directs plans and efforts. God was so unlimited, resourceful, clever, and not petty. She had to "unlearn" things to be open to other forms and tools that God uses. "It is perhaps obvious, but any form we use is helpful only in so far as it is helpful. They are not inherently sacred. God is sacred and develops new forms tailored to particular people and contexts--maybe he only uses them one time. Why should we assume the forms should be mass produced and have a certain shelf life? The God of platypuses and Venus flytraps is the God we serve. He is not some blazer-wearing CPA in the spiritual world trying to train other mini CPAs to apply codes. As Dallas used to say, 'He's a creator who creates creators.' God's kingdom has come to Atwater, whatever latitude and longitude we're at, and we have made distinction for our own purposes between spaces, but in reality this is God's world without distinction. So ministry is learning to live freely in a constant inflow and outflow of life with God and others through different spaces with the sole purpose of being present to listen, to love, and to be loved."

Cat's ministry embodies a concept central to Dr. Andrew Walls' writings on global Christianity. As Walls put it, Christians have to be willing to "live on someone else's terms." This approach to Christian ministry, while in the minority, has a good witness in Western Christianity. As Dr. Steven Bevans has written:

> A number of radical Christians, both Protestant and Catholic, eschewed the idea to extend Christendom and opted for another way of proclaiming Christ. While crusaders were 'prepared to compel,' missionaries opted against compulsion and attempted to 'demonstrate, invite, explain, entreat, and leave the results with God' . . . Since they could be heard only by communicating, women and men using the missionary mode needed to learn local languages, immerse themselves in culture, find a place in local society. While the crusade relied on power to bring people into Christendom, missionaries had to learn to 'live on terms set by other people.' Mission involves moving out of one's self and one's accustomed terrain and taking the risk of entering another world . . . as the Gospel itself is about God living on someone else's terms, the Word becoming flesh, divinity expressed in terms of humanity. And the

> transmission of the Gospel requires a process analogous, however distantly, to the great act on which the Christian faith depends.[17]

This more radical form of Christianity is essential to the future city of Los Angeles. L.A. needs a new Christian movement, not another institution. For it is when Christianity is a movement, before it takes institutional form, that Christianity is most effective. H. Richard Niebuhr once wrote, "Institutionalized Christianity, as it appears in denominations as well as in state churches, in liberal programs as well as in conservative creeds, is only a halting place between Christian movements."[18] He continues, "The Franciscan revolution not the Roman Catholic church, the Reformation not the Protestant churches, the Evangelical revival not the denominations which conserved its fruit-and denied it-show what Christianity really is."[19] When Christianity is working outside of the institutional box, as we see in Cat's ministry, Christianity can with "creative but responsible freedom," as David Bosch has written, "prolong the logic of the ministry of Jesus and the early church in an imaginative and creative way to our own time and context."[20]

Moore describes her ministry in this way: "Fostering community in social wastelands by practicing the art of friendship." Cat longs to meet others, human to human, in such spaces and watch God work through the relationship to transform, not only the other, but herself as well. To engage this ministry she moves toward the "liminal spaces," places of transition, of new beginnings, of both/and." She ministers in people's lives when they are at a crossroads, the place that Anthony Kiedis describes so powerfully in "Under the Bridge." Ministries like Cat Moore's and congregations like Erwin McManus' Mosaic express the best Christianity has to offer Los Angeles.

There continues to be a huge gap between dreams and reality in Los Angeles. Christianity's future city reminds us that we need not despair. In

Christ, the present state of the Rialto is no longer a portent of human dystopia but a fruitful tension between the "now and the not yet." It is a tension which motivates us to prayers and to action for the coming of the future city.

> I saw the Holy City, the New Jerusalem, coming down out of heaven from God . . . He will wipe every tear from their eyes. There will be no more death or mourning or crying or pain, for the old order of things has passed away. He who was seated on the throne said, 'I am making everything new!' - Revelation 21:2a, 4, 5a

This, then, is our way into the sunset. People will continue to come to Los Angeles to pursue their dreams. They may succeed. They may fail. Humans will continue to construct new ways of being and relating. Each with their own strengths and certainty. Each with their own blind spots and weaknesses. Christian institutions, based upon previous ways of being and relating, will struggle to survive. New Christian movements will adapt to new ways of life, creatively continuing the ministry of Jesus. Christianity in Los Angeles is an important part of this story. But L.A. or any other city, is not our ultimate destination. Our destination is the future city which comes down from heaven. This is the city where our wounds will be healed.

> Then the angel showed me the river of the water of life, as clear as crystal, flowing from the throne of God and of the Lamb down the middle of the great street of the city. On each side of the river stood the tree of life, bearing twelve crops of fruit, yielding its fruit every month. And the leaves of the tree are for the healing of the nations. No longer will there be any curse. -Revelation 22:1-3a

Come, Lord Jesus!

Lovejoy

Afterword

Pilgrimage in La La Land

They wanted to see everything with their own eyes and experience everything for themselves . . . [1]

Spiritual journeys are integral to Judeo-Christianity. From Abraham's journey from his hometown of Ur to Jesus' itinerant ministry in Israel, from Moses' journey to the Promised Land to Paul's apostolic ministry across the Mediterranean, travel for spiritual purposes is essential to the faith. Pilgrimage is again gaining popularity today.

In 476 A.D. the Roman emperor Romulus was overthrown by Odoacer, a German barbarian. The collapse of the Roman Empire and its storied "pax romana" had been on the horizon for decades. Roman citizens knew that dramatic change was coming. As early as 380 AD pilgrimage to the Holy Land was gaining popularity among Roman Christians.

In that same year, Etheria, a Christian woman from northern Europe, traveled to Jerusalem and other holy sites. She wrote her impressions in letters to fellow Christians back home.[2] Then Helena, the mother of Constantine, went on a widely publicized trip to Jerusalem. Her journey dramatically increased popular interest in pilgrimage.

Sociologist David Martin has written, "It is characteristic of contemporary spirituality to go more on real pilgrimages than to Church."[3] Rome was on the cusp of dramatic change in the late 4th century. Many sense that our culture is undergoing dramatic change in the 21st century. Perhaps pilgrimage can prepare us for the challenges of adapting to change.

Roman Christians engaged in pilgrimage to "express and renew their devotion to Christ by placing themselves at the geographical locations of major events in Christ's life."4 Others "adopted the life of continuous pilgrimage as a protest against a Christianity that had become socially acceptable and even, by the end of the fourth century, a convenient affiliation for the upwardly mobile."5

Western Christians might engage in pilgrimage in Los Angeles for similar purposes. Traveling to locations in Los Angeles to, as T.S. Eliot put it, "kneel where prayer has been valid," can draw out our own prayers of protest and renewal. Spending time removed from our daily habits and rhythms can bring the new energy and creativity needed for adaptation to an undefined future. As Martin has said, "dislocation to achieve relocation."6

I wrote this book in the hopes of stirring our holy imaginations. This appendix is another tool to help the reader in that regard. Below I have listed a number of resources, sites and tours that are available. I encourage you to focus on the stories of the book that have spoken most deeply to you and to develop "pilgrimages" that take you deeper into these spiritual stories.

Ready-Made Pilgrimages

1) St. Junipero Serra's Camino: A Pilgrimage Guide to the California Missions Franciscan Media Stephen J. Binz 2017

2) A Visit to Old Los Angeles and Environs by Brent C. Dickerson: http://web.csulb.edu/~odinthor/socal1.html

3) A Kids Tour of Sacred Places: https://www.laconservancy.org/sites/default/files/files/resources/citylife%20sacreds%20brochure%20.pdf

4) A Tour of Key Pentecostal Sites in Los Angeles by Dr. Mel Robeck http://www.randylovejoy.com/

"A La Carte" Resources for Developing Your Own Pilgrimages

1) Prayer Garden:
    Fuller Seminary: 135 N Oakland Ave, Pasadena, CA 91101

2) Spiritual Retreat Centers:

    St. Andrew's Abbey: 31001 N. Valyermo Rd., Valyermo, CA Phone: 661-944-2178

Web: https://www.saintandrewsabbey.com/

St. Matthew's Episcopal Church--a center for contemporary prayer: 1031 Bienveneda Ave., Pacific Palasades, CA Phone:310-454-1358 Web: http://www.stmatthews.com/

3) On-line Resources on Los Angeles

Randy Lovejoy.com: Los Angles timelines and more on God in the city. www.RandyLovejoy.com

Los Angeles Conservancy site:https://www.laconservancy.org/explore-la/historic-places

Los Angeles historic resources site: http://historicplacesla.org/

List of historic landmarks in L.A.:https://en.wikipedia.org/wiki/California_Historical_Landmarks_in_Los_Angeles_County

4) Printed Resources:
111 Places in Los Angeles That You Must Not Miss Moglen/Posey, Emons: Germany, 2017

Quiet Los Angeles Rebecca Razo, Frances Lincoln, China 2016 Discover Los Angeles Letitia Burns O'Conner, Getty: 1997

Sunset Boulevard: Cruising the Heart of Los Angeles Amy Dawes, Los Angeles Times books 2002

Finding Los Angeles by Foot: stair, street, bridge, pathway and Lane Bob Inman, Self-Published 2013

Endnotes

Chapter 1

[1] Baur J. E. (2010). *The Health Seekers of Southern California, 1879-1900*. Los Angeles: Huntington Library Press, p. 19.

[2] Early Christianity spread throughout the Mediterranean basin.

[3] Johnston, B.E. (1962). *California's Gabrielino Indians*. Los Angeles: Southwest Museum, 1962, pp. 1-5.

Lovejoy

[4] Ibid.

[5] Surls, R. & Gerber, J. (2016). *From Cows to Concrete: The Rise and Fall of Farming in Los Angeles.* Santa Monica: Angel City Press, 2016, p. 17.

[6] Hallenbeck, C. & Williams, J. H. (1938) *Legends of the Spanish Southwest.* Glendale: Arthur H. Clark Co., 1938, p. 311.

[7] Sturmberg, Robert, (1921). *History of San Antonio and of the early days in Texas San Antonio.* San Antonio: St. Joseph's Society Comp., as quoted in Hallenbeck and Cleve, p. 311.

[8] Colahan, C.A., (1994). *The Visions of Sor Maria de Agreda.* Tucson: University of Arizona Press, p. 96.

[9] Colahan, C. & Rodriguez, A. (1986). Relacion de Fray Francisco de Escobar del viaje desde el Reino de Nuevo Mexico haste eld Mar del Sur. *Missionalia Hispanica 43*, p. 67.

[10] Ibid., 66, 67.

[11] Ibid., 69.

[12] Plocheck, R. (2005). Franciscan Missionaries in Texas before 1690. *Texas Almanac.* Texas State Historical Association.

[13] Colahan, (1994). *The Visions of Sor Maria de Agreda*, p. 94.

[14] Hallenbeck & Williams., (1938). *Legends of the Spanish Southwest*, p. 96.

[15] Ibid.

[16] Colahan, & Rodriguez, (1986). Relacion de Fray Francisco de Escobar, pp. 373-394.

[17] James, G. W. (1904, April). The Founding of the Spanish Missions in California. *The Craftsman, VI*(1), 38-48. Retrieved from http://digicoll.library.wisc.edu/cgi-bin/DLDecArts/DLDecArts-idx?type=article&did=DLDecArts.hdv06n01.i0008&id=DLDecArts.hdv06n01&isize=M

[18] Palóu, F. (1955). Life of Fray Junipero Serra. *Academy of American Franciscan History. Documentary series, v. 3.* Washington: Academy of Amer. Franciscan Hist., pp. 110-111

[19] Hallenbeck & Williams, (1938). *Legends of the Spanish Southwest*, p. 313.

[20] These early Native American peoples, according to the theory, were part of a "Hokan speaking people."

[21] Wicher, E. (1927). *The Presbyterian Church in CA 1849-1927.* New York: The Grafton Press, p. 20.

[22] Hallenbeck & Williams., (1938). *Legends of the Spanish Southwest*, p. 311.

Chapter 2

[1] Phillips, J. & Phillips, M. (1963). California Dreamin' [recorded by The Mamas & The Papas] on *If You Can Believe Your Eyes and Ears* [vinyl record]. Hollywood, CA: Dunhill Records.

[2] Ulin, D. L. (2002). *Writing Los Angeles: A Literary Anthology.* New York: Literary Classics of the United States. pp. 53-54.

[3] Luther, C. (2011, January 23). "Jack LaLanne Obituary: Jack LaLanne Dies at 96; Spiritual Father of U.S. Fitness Movement". *Los Angeles Times.*

[4] Evanosky, D., & Kos, E. J. (2014). *Lost Los Angeles.* London: Pavilion. p. 6.

[5] Holiday, R. (2017, May 21). Loving Los Angeles: 36 Books to Help You Finally "Get" LA. Retrieved from https://ryanholiday.net/books-on-los-angeles/

[6] McWilliams, C. (1946). *Southern California Country: An Island on the Land.* New York: Duell, Sloan & Pearce. p. 376.

[7] Ulin, (2002), *Writing LA.* p. xv.

[8] Ibid., p. 284.

[9] Reid, D. (1994). *Sex, Death, and God in L.A.* Berkeley, CA: University of California Press. p. xxxiii

[10] Lewis, D. (2013, July 16). Thomas Edison Drove the Film Industry to California. Retrieved from http://mentalfloss.com/article/51722/thomas-edison-drove-film-industry-california

[11] Heimann, J. (2013). *Los Angeles. Portrait of a City*. Slovakia: Taschen. p. 9.

[12] Meares, H. (2013, March 08). Sign of the Times III: Henry C. Jensen, the Cunning Capitalist of L.A. Retrieved April 5, 2018, from https://www.kcet.org/history-society/sign-of-the-times-iii-henry-c-jensen-the-cunning-capitalist-of-la

[13] City of Los Angeles Department of Recreation & Parks. (n.d.). Retrieved April 06, 2018,   from https://web.archive.org/web/20100115220537/http://www.ci.la.ca.us/rap/dos/parks/griffithpk/gp_narrative.htm

[14] Ulin, (2002). *Writing L.A..*, p. 71.

[15] Heimann, (2013). *Los Angeles*, p. 9.

[16] Walt Disney. (2016, June 08). Retrieved from https://whenyouwishuponastarblog.wordpress.com/2016/06/08/walt-disney/

[17] Harari, Y. N. (2017). *Homo deus: A Brief History of Tomorrow*. New York: Harper. p. 35.

[18] Meares, (2013). Sign of the Times III.

[19] Ibid.

[20] Pronzini, B., & Adrian, J. (Eds.). (1995). *Hard-boiled: An Anthology of American Crime Stories*. Oxford: Oxford University Press. p. 169.

[21] Ulin., (2002), *Writing L.A.*, p. xvii

[22] Ibid.

[23] Ibid., p. 350.

Chapter 3

[1] Weist, The Reverend Derell T. (2009)., *Stories of the First Protestant Churches in Los Angeles: 1850-1880*. Self-Published., p. 5.

[2] Ibid.

[3] History of American Women Blog. *Biddy Mason.* (2017, April 02). Retrieved from http://www.womenhistoryblog.com/2013/05/biddy-mason.html

[4] She died with an estimated fortune of more than $300,000, the equivalent of $8,700,000 today. Ms. Mason was buried on January 15, 1891 having transcended so many of the social barriers in her day (in Evergreen Cemetery in the Boyle Heights neighborhood of Los Angeles).

[5] Galatians 3:28

[6] A mulatto is a person of mixed white and black ancestry, especially a person with one white and one black parent.

[7] Los Angeles Herald. (1907, October 20). J. L. Griffin Will Open Revival. *Los Angeles Herald.* Vol. 35, No. 18., Retrieved from https://cdnc.ucr.edu/cgi-bin/cdnc?a=d&d=LAH19071020.2.39&e=-------en--20--1--txt-txIN--------1.

[8] Williams died in 1969 and was buried in the Los Angeles National Cemetery.

[9] For an interesting overview on urban development see: https://placesjournal.org/article/downtown-a-short-history-of-american-urban-exceptionalism/

[10] See http://www.texasmonthly.com/the-culture/walker-railey/ and also http://articles.latimes.com/1992-08-26/local/me-6047_1_los-angeles-church

[11] See http://articles.latimes.com/1992-09-17/local/me-922_1_immanuel-presbyterian-church

[12] Immanuel Presbyterian Church Los Angeles (n.d.). Worship & Ministry Services. Retrieved from https://immanuelpres.org/en/

[13] Palma, K. (n.d.). Richard Allen: Apostle of Freedom. Retrieved from https://www.sutori.com/story/richard-allen-apostle-of-freedom-9d72ab14-2735-431a-9bdb-b58cb99f4b02

Chapter 4

[1] Surls & Gerber. (2016)., *From Cows to Concrete*, p.9.

[2] Brown, R. E. (1966). *The Gospel According to John* (Vol. 1). New York City: Doubleday., p. 33.

[3] Smith, D. M. (1974). *John*. Philadelphia: Fortress Press., p. 34.

[4] Walls, A. F. (2000, July). Eusebius Tries Again: Reconceiving the Study of Christian history. *International Bulletin of Missionary Research*, 24(3), p. 105.

[5] Morris, J., *Rolling Stone* (as cited in Ulin, D. L., *Writing L.A.*, (2002))., p. 597.

[6] Prescott, W. H. (1847). *Conquest of Peru*. New York: Hurst & Company., p. 189.

[7] Surls & Gerber. (2016)., *From Cows to Concrete*, p. 18.

[8] Wicher. (1927)., *The Presbyterian Church in California*, pp. 19-20.

[9] Webber, F. J. (1964). Book Review -The Pious Fund by Kenneth Johnson (Los Angeles: Dawson's Book Shop (1963)). Published in *Southern California Quarterly, 46*(1), pp. 93-94. Retrieved from http://scq.ucpress.edu/content/ucpsocal/46/1/93.full.pdf

[10] The Tongva named changed as a result of their association with the San Gabriel Arcangel Mission.

[11] Surls & Gerber (2016)., *From Cows to Concrete*, p. 19.

[12] Wicher. (1927)., *The Presbyterian Church in California*.

[13] Speer, R. E. (1904). *Missions and Modern History, Vol. 1 of 2: A Study of the Missionary Aspects of Some Great Movements of the Nineteenth Century*. Grand Rapids, MI: Fleming H. Revell Company., p. 87.

[14] Restall & Fernandez-Armesto. (2012)., *The Conquistadors*, p. 90.

[15] Wicher. (1927)., *The Presbyterian Church in California*, p. 20.

[16] Latourette, K. S. (1969). *A History of the Expansion of Christianity* (Vol. 4). New York City: Harper & Row., pp. 303-304.

[17] In 1795 Fages gave 6,647-acres to another soldier, José Vicente Feliz. Rancho Los Feliz includes Los Feliz and Griffith Park, and was bounded on the east by the Los Angeles River.

[18] Surls & Gerber. (2016)., *From Cows to Concrete*, p. 35.

[19] Reid, H., & Heizer, R. F. (1968). *The Indians of Los Angeles County: Hugo Reid's Letters of 1852. Edited and annotated by Robert F. Heizer.* Los Angeles: Southwest Museum Papers No. 21. The land grant, which covered parts of what is now Arcadia, Monrovia, Sierra Madre, Pasadena, and San Marino was recognized by Governor Pio Pico in 1845.

[20] A small portion of the rancho has been preserved as the Los Angeles County Arboretum and Botanic Garden.

[21] Surls & Gerber (2016)., *From Cows to Concrete*, p. 33.

[22] Engh, M. E. (1992)., *Frontier Faiths*, p. 172.

[23] See Pitt, L. (1998). *The Decline of the Californios: A Social History of the Spanish-speaking Californians, 1846-1890.* Berkeley, CA: University of California Press.

[24] During the Mexican-American War, Lugo led a militia of the Californio, on the Mexican side. In that role, in 1846, he was ordered to punish a band of Luiseno Indians. The Indians had killed 11 Californio lancers in revenge for horses that had been stolen from them in the Pauma Massacre. He and his militia, together with their allies the Cahuilla Indians, killed 33-40 Luiseno in another massacre, the Temecula Massacre.

[25] Spencer, T. (1978, November 15). Compton's historic tree has fallen far from glory days. *Los Angeles Times*, p. 73.

[26] Surls & Gerber (2016)., *From Cows to Concrete*, p. 38.

[27] Manifest Destiny is 19th-century belief that the expansion of the US American was justified and inevitable.

[28] The park called the Fletcher Brown Square.

[29] Surls & Gerber (2016)., *From Cows to Concrete*, pp. 39-40.

[30] Wiest (2009)., *Stories of the First Protestant Churches in L.A.*, p. 1.

[31] Wiest (2009)., *Stories of the First Protestant Churches in L.A.*, p. 19.

[32] Feldman, F. L. (2003). Human Services in the City of Angels Part I: 1850-1920. *Southern California Quarterly, 85*(2)., p. 159.

[33] St. John de Crèvecoeur, J. Hector, J. H. (1963). *Letters from an American Farmer and Sketches of Eighteenth-century America; More Letters from an American Farmer.* New York: American Library.

[34] Coan, T. M. (1875, April). A New Country. *The Galaxy.* p. 463.

[35] Adams, J. T. (1831). *Epic of America.* Boston: Little, Brown, and Co., p. 214.

[36] Bartlett, D. W. (1907). *The Better City: A Sociological Study of a Modern City.* Los Angeles: The Neuner Company Press., p. 215.

[37] Feldman. (2003). Human Services in the City of Angels, p. 159.

[38] Ibid, p. 195.

[39] Ibid.

[40] O'Conner, L. B. (1997). *Discovering Los Angeles: An Informed Guide to L.A.'s Right and Varied Cultural Life.* Los Angeles: J. Paul Getty Trust., p. 140.

[41] For more on Andrew Wall's distinction between proselytism and conversion see: Walls, A. F. (1997). *The Missionary Movement in Christian History: Studies in the Transmission of Faith.* Maryknoll, NY: Orbis Books., pp. 51-53. Also see: Burrows, W. R., Gornik, M. R., & McLean, J. A. (2011). *Understanding World Christianity: The Vision and Work of Andrew F. Walls.* Maryknoll, NY: Orbis Books., pp. 131-135.

[42] Barragan, B. (2014, June 25). Silver Lake Church-to-Hotel Conversion Finally Moving Forward. Retrieved from https://la.curbed.com/2014/6/25/10083320/silver-lake-churchtohotel-conversion-finally-moving-forward

Chapter 5

[1] Morris, J., Los Angeles: The Know-How City. *Rolling Stone* (as cited in Ulin, D. L., *Writing L.A.*, (2002))., p. 612.

[2] Ulin, D. L..(2002)., *Writing L.A.*, p. xiv.

[3] Sahagun, L. (2013, October 28). The L.A. Aqueduct at 100. Retrieved from http://graphics.latimes.com/me-aqueduct/

[4] Ibid.

[5] Kegley, H. (1930, June 29). Venice Battle Attests Oil and Water Do Mix. *Los Angeles Times*.

[6] Fuller, D. P. (1972). *Give the Winds a Mighty Voice: The Story of Charles E. Fuller*. New York City: Word., p. 75.

[7] Ibid. p. 76.

[8] Ibid. p. 238.

[9] Dochuk, D. (2012). *From Bible Belt to Sunbelt: Plain Folk Religion, Grassroots Politics, and the Rise of the Conservative Southwest."* New York City: W. W. Norton & Company.

[10] Graham, B. (1997). *Just As I Am: The Autobiography of Billy Graham*. San Francisco: Zondervan., p. 145.

[11] Ibid. p. 145.

[12] For more see: Mears, H. C. (2012). *Dream Big: The Henrietta Mears Story*. Delight, AR: Gospel Light.

[13] Anderson, H. A. (2010, June 15). "Hamblen, Carl Stuart." Retrieved from *Handbook of Texas Online*, http://www.tshaonline.org/handbook/online/articles/fhafq

[14] Bartlett, D. W. (1907)., *The Better City*, p. 248.

[15] Reznikoff, C. (1941). "Rainy Season." *Autobiography: Hollywood* as quoted in Ulin, D. L., (2002)., *Writing L.A.*, p. 271.

[16] See Issenberg, S. (2008, June 8). "RFK's Death Now Viewed as First Case of Mideast Violence Exported to U.S." *San Diego Union Tribune (Boston Globe)*. Retrieved from http://legacy.sandiegouniontribune.com/uniontrib/20080608/news_1n8rfk.html

[17] Cudd, A. E. (2006). *Analyzing Oppression*. New York: Oxford University Press.

[18] Wolf, A. (1992). "Bibliography of Exclusion and Embrace." From Lamont, M., & Fournier, M. (Eds.). (1992). *Cultivating Differences: Symbolic Boundaries and the Making of Inequality*. Chicago: University of Chicago Press., p. 309.

[19] Stevenson, B. E. (2015). *The Contested Murder of Latasha Harlins: Justice, Gender, and the Origins of the LA Riots*. Oxford, England, UK: Oxford University Press.

[20] Soja, E. W. (2014). *My Los Angeles: From Urban Restructuring to Regional Urbanization*. Berkeley, California: Univ. of California Press. Excerpts from Chapter 1.

[21] Video of the facility: https://www.youtube.com/watch?v=vwLq375IEJI

[22] HLC Filming and Events. (2014, June 16). Immanuel Presbyterian Church (Tour). Retrieved April 11, 2018, from https://www.youtube.com/watch?v=vwLq375IEJI 2

Chapter 6

[1] King, Jr., M.L. (1963). "Letter from Birmingham Jail." *Liberation: An Independent Monthly*. Vol. 8 no. 4. pp. 10–16, 23.

[2] Definition of Hagiography: "A biography of saints or venerated persons" from Hagiography. (2018, March 23). Retrieved from https://www.merriam-webster.com/dictionary/hagiography

[3] Vandersloot, J. D. (1988, September 11). The Charges Against Father Junipero Serra. *Los Angeles Times*. Retrieved from http://articles.latimes.com/1988-09-11/local/me-2801_1_father-serra-mission-system-san-juan-capistrano-mission

[4] Rimbert, E. (1998, May 30). Junipero Serra Statue Unveiled and Blessed. *Los Angeles Times*. Retrieved from http://articles.latimes.com/1998/may/30/local/me-54783

5 In 2006, California lawmakers voted to replace Thomas Starr King's statue with a statue of President Ronald Reagan. King's statue was moved to Sacramento, the California state capitol. See: Kennedy, G. (2009, December 21). A Giant of California History Returns to Sacramento. *Los Angeles Times.* Retrieved from http://articles.latimes.com/2009/dec/21/local/la-me-beliefs21-2009dec21

6 Frankiel, S. S. (1988). *California's Spiritual Frontiers: Religious Alternatives in Anglo-Protestantism; 1850-1910.* Berkeley, Calif.: Univ. of California Pr., p. 18.

7 Frankiel, S. S. (1988)., *California's Spiritual Frontiers*, p. 30. A few definitions of Theological liberalism may be helpful here: 1) "Theological liberalism is a kind of consecration of all the best ethics and science and philosophy regarded as the manifestation of the will of God to man," 2) "all claims to truth, in theology as in other disciplines, must be made on the basis of reason and experience, not by appeal to external authority." From Dorrien, G. J. (2001). *The Making of American Liberal Theology: Imagining Progressive Religion, 1805--1900.* Louisville, Kentucky: Westminster John Knox Press., p. 1.

8 "He was indeed a very active Presbyterian layman, and was courted by mission board executives, especially Robert Speer." From Sandeen, E. R. (2008). *The Roots of Fundamentalism: British and American Millenarianism, 1800-1930* (Reprint Edition ed.). Chicago: University of Chicago Press., p. 193.

9 Sandeen, E. R. (2008). *The Roots of Fundamentalism: British and American Millenarianism, 1800-1930* (Reprint Edition ed.). Chicago: University of Chicago Press., p. 4.

10 Ibid., p. 193-194. In February of that same year, Stewart published the first volume of "The Fundamentals."

11 Ibid., p. 119. Two definitions of Fundamentalism: 1) As historian George Marsden describes it, "fundamentalists shared with the discontented intellectuals of the 1920s, if little else, a sense of profound spiritual and cultural crisis of the twentieth century." He continues, "Unlike their more disillusioned contemporaries, however, they had very definite ideas of where things had gone wrong. Modernism and the theory of solution, they were convinced, had caused the catastrophe by undermining the Biblical foundations of American civilization." 2) "Militantism is what set fundamentalism off

from a number of closely related traditions, such as evangelicalism, revivalism, pietism, the holiness movements, millenarianism, Reformed confessionalism, Baptist traditionalism, and other denominational orthodoxies." Sandeen, E. R. (2008)., p. 3-4.

[12] Walls, A. F. (2002). *The Missionary Movement in Christian History: Studies in the Transmission of Faith.* Maryknoll, New York: Orbis Books., p. 8.

[13] Barth, K. (1968). *The Epistle to the Romans.* Oxford: Oxford University Press., p. 104

[14] Gutting, G. (2005). *Foucault: A Very Short Introduction.* Oxford: Oxford University Press., p. 50.

[15] Matthew, Chapter 1 (TNIV version)

[16] Brown, E. (2015, July 21). Native American Origins: When the DNA Points Two Ways. Retrieved from http://www.latimes.com/science/sciencenow/la-sci-sn-native-american-origins-dna-20150721-story.html

[17] Restall, M., & Fernandez-Armesto, F. (2012). *The Conquistadors.* Oxford: Oxford Univ. Press., p. 8.

[18] Ibid., p. 94.

[19] In a historical moment reminiscent of the derivation of the word Barbarian. It was originally coined by Greeks to refer to non-Greeks. The term means "babblers."

[20] Caughey, L., & Caughey, J. (Eds.). (1977). *Los Angeles: Biography of a City.* Berkeley (Calif.): University of California Press., pp. 41-42.

[21] Smith, G. A., & Walker, C. (1965). *Indian Slave Trade along the Mojave Trail.* San Bernardino: San Bernardino County Museum.

[22] Caughey, L., & Caughey, J. (Eds.). (1977)., *Los Angeles*, p.42.

[23] Evanosky, D., & Kos, E. J. (2014). *Lost Los Angeles.* London: Pavilion., p. 11

[24] Kroeber, A. L. (1925). *Handbook of the Indians of California.* North Clemsford, MA: Courier Corporation.

[25] Bolton, H. E., (1930). Diary of Pedro Font. *Anza's California Expeditions, Vol. IV.* Berkeley (Calif.): University of California Press., pp. 174-182.

[26] Latourette, K. S. (1969). *A History of the Expansion of Christianity (Vol. 3).* New York City: Harper & Row., p. 88.

[27] Latourette, K. S. (1969)., *A History of the Expansion of Christianity,* p. 89.

[28] Speer, R. E. (1904). *Missions and Modern History,* p. 187.

[29] Dumont, J. (1997). *El amanecer de los derechos del hombre: La controversia de Valladolid.* Madrid: Ediciones Encuentro.

[30] Butler, W. (1893). *Mexico in transition, from the power of political Romanism to civil and religious liberty.* New York: Hunt & Eaton., p. 189

[31] Nash, E. (2005, January 29). Don Quixote: The unlikely conquistador. Retrieved from https://www.independent.co.uk/arts-entertainment/books/features/don-quixote-the-unlikely-conquistador-488736.html

[32] Saavedra, M. D. (1995). *The history of that ingenious gentleman, Don Quijote de la Mancha* (B. Raffel, Trans.). New York: Norton., p. 43.

[33] Nash, E. (2005). Don Quixote.

[34] Speer, R. E. (1904). *Missions and Modern History,* p. 489.

[35] Palou's *Relacion historica de la vida y apostolic areas del venerable padre fray Junipero Serra* published in Mexico City in 1787, is an early example of the genre of literature used by the Catholic church for this purpose.

[36] Thomas Heffernan, in his book "Sacred Biography" points out that hagiography was concerned not only with the saint's life but also with the "meta historical," that is, the divine indwelling in that person.

[37] Caughey, L., & Caughey, J. (Eds.). (1977). *Los Angeles: Biography of a City.* Berkeley (Calif.): University of California Press., pp. 241-242.

[38] Caughey, L., & Caughey, J. (Eds.). (1977)., p.240.

39 Himmelfarb, G. (1987). *The New History and the Old: Critical Essays and Reappraisals*. Cambridge (Mass.): Harvard University Press., p. 35.

40 Wicher, E. A. (1927). *The Presbyterian Church in California, 1849-1927*. New York: F.H. Hitchcock., p. 18.

41 Rønde, J. (Director). (2016, June 27). *The DNA Journey feat. Carlos* [Video file]. Retrieved from https://www.youtube.com/watch?v=EYnutforqeY

42 King, Jr., M.L. (1963). "Letter from Birmingham Jail". *Liberation: An Independent Monthly*. Vol. 8 no. 4. pp. 10–16, 23.

Chapter 7

1 Inscription on a plaque at the entrance of Berendo Street Korean Baptist Church in Los Angeles. July 31, 1977

2 Acts 1:8

3 Acts 2:5-12

4 Ulin, D. L. (2002)., *Writing L.A.*, quoting Pico Iyer., p. 830.

5 Rieff, D. (1992). *Los Angeles: Capital of the Third World*. New York City: Touchstone., p. 239.

6 Rieff, D. (1992)., *L.A.*, p. 329.

7 Yeretzian, A. S., *A History of Armenian Immigration to America with Special Reference to Los Angeles*. San Francisco: R. & E. Research Associates, 94112 Library of Congress # 73-824000: University of Southern California (1974)., p. 7. (Reprinted from *A History of Armenian Immigration to America with Special Reference to Los Angeles* (Master's thesis, University of Southern California). Los Angeles: University of Southern California, (1923)).

8 Barton, J. L. (2007). *Daybreak in Turkey*. Whitefish, Montana: Kessinger Publishing, LLC., p. 7.

9 Shenk, W. R., & Plantinga, R. J. (Eds.). (2016). *Christianity & Religious Plurality: Historical and Global Perspectives*. Eugene, Oregon: Cascade Books, an imprint of Wipf and Stock., p. 266.

[10] Salem is the pre-Israelite name for the city we call Jerusalem

[11] Joshua 24:2; Genesis 12.

[12] Cyrus and the Empire also appear in the biblical book of Isaiah: "I will raise up Cyrus in my righteousness: I will make all his ways straight. He will rebuild my city and set my exiles free, but not for a price or reward, says the Lord Almighty" Isaiah 45:13.

[13] Arshagouni, H., & Arshagouni, M. (1998). *Armenian Time Line*. Mission Hills, California: Ararat Home of Los Angeles., p. 7.

[14] Latourette, K. S. (1969). *A History of the Expansion of Christianity (Vol. 1)*. New York City: Harper & Row., p. 231.

[15] Kelley, R., Friedlander, J., & Colby, A. Y. (Eds.). (1993). *Irangeles: Iranians in Los Angeles*. Berkeley, California: University of California Press., p. 65.

[16] Ibid.

[17] Rashidvash, V. (2013). Iranian People: Iranian Ethnic Groups. *International Journal of Humanities and Social Science, 3*(15), 216-226. Retrieved from http://www.ijhssnet.com/journals/Vol_3_No_15_August_2013/24.pdf

[18] Der-Martirosian, C. (2008). *Iranian Immigrants in Los Angeles: The Role of Networks and Economic Integration*. New York City: LFB Scholarly Publishing LLC., p. 111.

[19] Speer, R. E. (1904). *Missions and Modern History, Vol. 2 of 2: A Study of the Missionary Aspects of Some Great Movements of the Nineteenth Century*. Grand Rapids, MI: Fleming H. Revell Company., p. 444.

[20] Speer, R. E. (1904)., *Missions and Modern History*, p. 459.

[21] Bournoutian, G. A. (1993). *A History of the Armenian People 1500 AD to the Present* (Vol. II). Costa Meza, California: Mazda., p. 189.

[22] Most Armenians in Los Angeles, for example, are part of the Armenian Apostolic Church. St. Mary's in Glendale is the religious hub of Armenian Iranian Community p. 121

[23] Yu, E., Phillips, E. H., & Yang, E. S. (Eds.). (1982). *Koreans in Los Angeles: Prospects and Promises*. Los Angeles: Koryo Research Institute., p. 5.

[24] Speer, R. E. (1904)., *Missions and Modern History*, p. 360.

[25] Griffis, W. E. (1884). *Korea: The Hermit Nation*. New York: C. Scribners Sons., Ch. 5. p. xliv-xlvi.

[26] Yu, et al.(1982). *Koreans in Los Angeles*, p. 5.

[27] Yu, et al.(1982). *Koreans in Los Angeles*, p. 2.

[28] Shenk, W. R., & Plantinga, R. J. (Eds.). (2016). *Christianity & Religious Plurality: Historical and Global perspectives*. Eugene, Oregon: Cascade Books, an imprint of Wipf and Stock., p. 269.

[29] Ibid.

[30] A & E. (2017, April 18). L.A. Burning: The Riots 25 Years Later. Retrieved from https://www.youtube.com/watch?v=OCYT9Hew9ZU

[31] Lah, K. (2017, April 29). The L.A. Riots were a Rude Awakening for Korean Americans. Retrieved from https://www.cnn.com/2017/04/28/us/la-riots-korean-americans/index.html

[32] Ibid.

[33] Takaki, R. T. (1998). *Strangers from a Different Shore: A History of Asian Americans*. Boston: Little, Brown and Co., p. 193.

[34] Takaki, R. T. (1998)., *Strangers from a Different Shore*, p. 388.

[35] Ibid. p. 380.

[36] Rieff, D. (1992)., *L.A.*, p. 163.

[37] Latourette, K. S. (1969). *A History of the Expansion of Christianity (Vol. 3)*. New York City: Harper & Row., pp. 323-324.

[38] Okada, V. N. (1998). *Triumphs of Faith: Stories of Japanese-American Christians During World War II*. Los Angeles: Japanese_American Internment Project., p. 27.

[39] Kurashige, S. (2008). *The Shifting Grounds of Race: Black and Japanese Americans in the Making of Multiethnic Los Angeles*. Princeton, New Jersey: Princeton University Press., p. 168.

[40] Latourette, K. S. (1969). *A History of the Expansion of Christianity (Vol. 3)*. New York City: Harper & Row., p. 361.

[41] Ibid., pp. 361-362.

[42] Ibid., p. 362.

[43] Ibid.

[44] Shin, S., & Ahn-Park, Y. (2017, January 13). Why Are There So Many Korean Missionaries in the U.S., a "Missionaries' Nation"? *The Kukmin Daily*. Retrieved from http://www.kukmindaily.co.kr/article/view.asp?arcid=0011197657

[45] Shenk, W. R., & Plantinga, R. J. (Eds.). (2016). *Christianity & Religious Plurality*. p. 262.

[46] Allen, L. C. (2015). *Word Biblical Commentary: Psalms 101-150* (Vol. 21, World Biblical Commentary). Grand Rapids, Michigan: Zondervan., p. 113.

[47] Hebrews 5:11-10:39

[48] Volf, M. (2017). *Flourishing: Why We Need Religion in a Globalized World*. New Haven, Connecticut: Yale University Press. (Mt. 7:12)., p. 150.

[49] Bauckham, R. (1993). *The Theology of the Book of Revelation (New Testament Theology)*. Cambridge: Cambridge University Press., p. 161.

[50] Shenk, W. R., & Plantinga, R. J. (Eds.). (2016). *Christianity & religious plurality*. p. 273.

Chapter 8

[1] Sherwood, Y. (2012). Jonah and Jesus. *Sh'ma: A Journal of Jewish Ideas*, (Sept. 3), p. 8. Retrieved from http://shma.com/2012/09/jonah-and-jesus/

² Seymour, W. J., & Martin, L. E. (2000). *The Doctrines and Discipline of the Azusa Street Apostolic Faith Mission of Los Angeles, California.* Joplin, MO: Christian Life Books, the Publishing arm of River of Revival Ministries. As reproduced in Espinosa, G. (2014). *William J. Seymour and the Origins of Global Pentecostalism: A Biography and Documentary History.* Durham, North Carolina: Duke University Press., p. 228.

³ This group later becoming the Church of God, Anderson, Indiana.

⁴ Robeck, C. M. (2006). *The Azusa Street Mission and Revival: The Birth of the Global Pentecostal Movement.* Nashville, Tennessee: Thomas Nelson., p. 30.

⁵ Scientists have described speaking in tongues, or glossolalia, as verbalized religious experience with only a few vowels and consonants. See Parham, Sarah E. (1969). *The Life of Charles F. Parham.* Joplin, MO: Press of the Hunter Printing Company., p. 42.

⁶ Robeck, C. M. (2006)., *The Azusa Street Mission and Revival*, p. 9.

⁷ Pre-millenialism seems to have been the dominant view in the first three centuries of Christianity and holds that certain signs, such as the preaching of the gospel to all nations, must occur before the return of Christ and 1,000 years of peace and righteousness. Other options include post-millenialism which holds that the Kingdom of God is now being extended through Christian teaching and preaching and a-millenialism which holds that the Bible does not predict a period of peace and righteousness before the end of the world. See Clouse, R. G., & Ladd, G. E. (1987). *The Meaning of the Millennium: Four Views.* Downers Grove, Illinois: InterVarsity Press.

⁸ Acts 2:4 (TNIV) reads... "All of them were filled with the Holy Spirit and began to speak in other tongues as the Spirit enabled them."

⁹ See chapter 3.

¹⁰ Robeck, C. M. (2006)., *The Azusa Street Mission and Revival*, p. 314.

¹¹ Anderson, G. H. (1999). *Biographical Dictionary of Christian Missions.* Grand Rapids, Michigan: W.B. Eerdmans Pub., p. 613.

¹² Plot Number 3332 in Evergreen Cemetery in the Boyle Heights neighborhood of Los Angeles (same cemetery where Biddy Mason is buried).

[13] Robeck, C. M. (2006)., *The Azusa Street Mission and Revival*, p. 320.

[14] Summerfield, H., Ryken, L. & Eldredge, L. (2009). "Jonah". Jeffrey, D. L. (Ed.). *A Dictionary of Biblical Tradition in English Literature*. Grand Rapids, MI: W.B. Eerdmans., pp. 409-411.

[15] Rad, G. V. (1965). *The Message of the Prophets*. San Francisco: HarperCollins, LLC., p. 256.

[16] See Acts chapter 2

[17] Chryssides, G. D. (2011). *Historical Dictionary of New Religious Movements* (2nd ed., Historical Dictionaries of Religions, Philosophies, and Movements). Lanham, Maryland: The Scarecrow Press., p. 14.

[18] Quoted in Sherrill, J. L. (1965). *They Speak with Other Tongues*. Ada, Michigan: Revell Publishing., p. 101.

[19] Chryssides, G. D. (2011)., *Historical Dictionary of New Religious Movements*, p. 14.

[20] The Welsh Revival of 1904-1905--Truth in History. (n.d.). Retrieved August 23, 2018, from http://truthinhistory.org/the-welsh-revival-of-1904-1905-2.html

[21] See Orr, J. E. (1975). *The Flaming Tongue: Evangelical Awakenings, 1900-*. Chicago: Moody Press.

[22] Smale, J., & Welch, T. (2017). *The Pentecostal Blessing: Sermons That Prepared Los Angeles for the Azusa Street Revival* (Spirit Empowered) (C. M. Robeck Jr. & D. Rodgers, Eds.). Springfield, Missouri: Gospel Publishing House.

[23] Owens, R. R. (2005). *The Azusa Street Revival: Its Roots and Its Message*. Maitland, Florida: Xulon Press.

[24] Ibid.

[25] Anderson, G. H. (1999)., *Biographical Dictionary of Christian Missions*, p. 236.

[26] Ibid.

[27] Mcgee, G. B. (1999). William J. Seymour and the Azusa Street Revival. *The Enrichment Journal*,(Fall)., p. 2. Retrieved from http://enrichmentjournal.ag.org/199904/026_azusa.cfm

[28] Taylor, J. V. (2004). *The Go-between God (2nd Edi*tion). London: SCM Press., p. 198.

[29] Adams, D. (1986). *The Hitchhikers Guide to the Galaxy*. New York: Harmony Books.

[30] Sassoon, J. M. (1995). *Jonah* (The Anchor Yale Bible Commentaries). New Haven, Connecticut: Yale University Press., p. 320.

[31] Feinstein, E. (2012). How can you sleep? *Sh'ma A Journal of Jewish Ideas*. Retrieved from http://shma.com/2012/09/how-can-you-sleep/

[32] Seymour, W. J., & Martin, L. E. (2000). *Doctrines and Discipline of Azusa Street Apostolic Faith Mission*, p. 228

Chapter 9

[1] Newbigin, L. (1981). *Sign of the Kingdom*. Grand Rapids, Michigan: Eerdmans., p. 49.

[2] Löwith, K. (1957). *Meaning in History: The Theological Implications of the Philosophy of History*. Chicago: University of Chicago Press., p. 185.

[3] Newbigin, L. (1981)., *Sign of the Kingdom*, p. 49.

[4] Volf, M. (2017). *Flourishing: Why We Need Religion in a Globalized World* (Reprint ed.). New Haven, Connecticut: Yale University Press., p. 61.

[5] Niebuhr, H. R. (1988). *The Kingdom of God in America*. Middletown, Connecticut: Wesleyan Univ. Press., p. xv.

[6] Die Predigt Jesu vom Reiche Gottes ("Jesus' Proclamation of the Kingdom of God"), 1892.

[7] Bauckham, R. (1993)., p. 12.

[8] Newbigin, L., & Weston, P. (2006). *Lesslie Newbigin: Missionary Theologian: A Reader*. Grand Rapids, Michigan: Eerdmans Pub., p. 216.

[9] Barth, K. (1968). *The Epistle to the Romans* (E. C. Hoskyns, Trans.). Oxford: Oxford University Press., p. 104.

[10] Walls, A. F. (2002). *The Missionary Movement in Christian History: Studies in the Transmission of Faith*. Maryknoll, New York: Orbis Books., p. 22.

[11] Bauckham, R. (1993)., *Theology of the Book of Revelation*, p. 129.

[12] Martin, D. (2008). *Sacred History and Sacred Geography: Spiritual Journeys in Time and Space*. Vancouver: Regent College., p. 11.

[13] Bauckham, R. (1993)., *Theology of the Book of Revelation*, p. 130.

[14] Dunn, J. D. (1997). *Jesus and the Spirit: A Study of the Religious and Charismatic Experience of Jesus and the First Christians as Reflected in the New Testament*. Grand Rapids, Michigan: Eerdmans., p. 360.

[15] (2017, October 13). The Story Behind RHCP's 'Under the Bridge'. Retrieved August 23, 2018, from https://www.ultimate-guitar.com/articles/features/the_story_behind_rhcps_under_the_bridge-67557

[16] Kiedis, A., with Flea, Frusciante, J., & Smith, C. (1992). Under the Bridge [Recorded by Red Hot Chili Peppers]. On *Blood Sugar Sex Magik* [Vinyl recording]. Los Angeles: Warner Brothers.

[17] Burrows, W. R., Gornik, M. R., & McLean, J. A. (2011). *Understanding World Christianity: The Vision and Work of Andrew F. Walls*. Maryknoll, New York: Orbis Books., pp. 130-131.

[18] Niebuhr, H. R. (1988)., *Kingdom of God in America*, p. xiv.

[19] Ibid.

[20] Bosch, D. J. (1991). *Transforming Mission: Paradigm Shifts in Theology of Mission*. Maryknoll, New York: Orbis Books., p. 181.

Afterword

Lovejoy

[1] Schaff, P., & Wace, H. (1893). *A Select Library of the Nicene and Post-Nicene Fathers of the Christian Church: Volume VI, St. Jerome: Letters and Select Works* (Vol. VI, Second). New York City: Christian Literature., Ep. 108.9.

[2] Miles, M. R. (1990). *Practicing Christianity: Critical Perspectives for an Embodied Spirituality*. New York, New York: The Crossroads Publishing Company, p. 43.

[3] Martin, D. (2008). *Sacred History and Sacred Geography: Spiritual Journeys in Time and Space*. Vancouver: Regent College., p. 25.

[4] Miles, M. R. (2006)., *Practicing Christianity*, p. 44.

[5] Ibid.

[6] Martin, D. (2008)., *Sacred History and Sacred Geography*, p. 30.

Bibliography

Adams, D. (1986). *The Hitchhikers Guide to the Galaxy*. New York: Harmony Books.

A & E. (2017, April 18). L.A. Burning: The Riots 25 Years Later. Retrieved from https://www.youtube.com/watch?v=OCYT9Hew9ZU

Allen, L. C. (2015). *Word Biblical Commentary: Psalms 101-150* (Vol. 21, World Biblical Commentary). Grand Rapids, Michigan: Zondervan.

Anderson, A. (2013). *To the Ends of the Earth: Pentecostalism and the Transformation of World Christianity* (First ed., Oxford Studies in World Christianity). New York City: Oxford University Press.

Anderson, G. H. (1999). *Biographical Dictionary of Christian Missions*. Grand Rapids, Michigan: W.B. Eerdmans Publishing.

Anderson, H. A. (2010, June 15). "Hamblen, Carl Stuart." Retrieved from *Handbook of Texas Online*, http://www.tshaonline.org/handbook/online/articles/fhafq

Arshagouni, H., & Arshagouni, M. (1998). *Armenian Time Line*. Mission Hills, California: Ararat Home of Los Angeles.

Barragan, B. (2014, June 25). Silver Lake Church-to-Hotel Conversion Finally Moving Forward. Retrieved from https://la.curbed.com/2014/6/25/10083320/silver-lake-churchtohotel-conversion-finally-moving-forward

Barth, K. (1968). *The Epistle to the Romans*. Oxford: Oxford University Press.

Bartlett, D. W. (1907). *The Better City: A Sociological Study of a Modern City*. Los Angeles: The Neuner Company Press.

Barton, J. L. (2007). *Daybreak in Turkey*. Whitefish, Montana: Kessinger Publishing, LLC.

Bauckham, R. (1993). *The Theology of the Book of Revelation (New Testament Theology)*. Cambridge: Cambridge University Press.

Baur J. E. (2010). *The Health Seekers of Southern California, 1879-1900*. Los Angeles: Huntington Library Press.

Bolton, H. E., (1930). Diary of Pedro Font. *Anza's California Expeditions, Vol. IV*. Berkeley (Calif.): University of California Press.

Bosch, D. J. (1991). *Transforming Mission: Paradigm Shifts in Theology of Mission*. Maryknoll, New York: Orbis Books.

Bournoutian, G. A. (1993). *A History of the Armenian People 1500 AD to the Present* (Vol. II). Costa Meza, California: Mazda.

Brown, E. (2015, July 21). Native American Origins: When the DNA Points Two Ways. Retrieved from http://www.latimes.com/science/sciencenow/la-sci-sn-native-american-origins-dna-20150721-story.html

Brown, R. E. (1966). *The Gospel According to John* (Vol. 1). New York City: Doubleday.

Burrows, W. R., Gornik, M. R., & McLean, J. A. (2011). *Understanding World Christianity: The Vision and Work of Andrew F. Walls*. Maryknoll, New York: Orbis Books.

Butler, W. (1893). *Mexico in Transition: From the Power of Political Romanism to Civil and Religious Liberty*. New York: Hunt & Eaton.

Caughey, L., & Caughey, J. (Eds.). (1977). *Los Angeles: Biography of a City*. Berkeley (Calif.): University of California Press.

Chryssides, G. D. (2011). *Historical Dictionary of New Religious Movements* (2nd ed., Historical Dictionaries of Religions, Philosophies, and Movements). Lanham, Maryland: The Scarecrow Press.

City of Los Angeles Department of Recreation & Parks. (n.d.). Retrieved from https://web.archive.org/web/20100115220537/http://www.ci.la.ca.us/rap/dos/parks/griffithpk/gp_narrative.htm

Coan, T. M. (1875, April). A New Country. *The Galaxy*.

Colahan, C. A. (1994). *The Visions of Sor Mari´ a de Agreda*. The University of Arizona Press.

Colahan, C. & Rodriguez, A. (1986). Relacion de Fray Francisco de Escobar del viaje desde el Reino de Nuevo Mexico haste eld Mar del Sur. *Missionalia Hispanica 43.*

Cudd, A. E. (2006). *Analyzing Oppression.* New York: Oxford University Press.

Dana, R. H. (1840). *Two Years Before the Mast.* New York: Harper and Brothers.

Der-Martirosian, C. (2008). *Iranian Immigrants in Los Angeles: The Role of Networks and Economic Integration.* New York City: LFB Scholarly Publishing LLC.

Dochuk, D. (2012). *From Bible Belt to Sunbelt: Plain Folk Religion, Grassroots Politics, and the Rise of the Conservative Southwest."* New York City: W. W. Norton & Company.

Dumont, J. (1997). *El amanecer de los derechos del hombre: La controversia de Valladolid.* Madrid: Ediciones Encuentro.

Dunn, J. D. (1997). *Jesus and the Spirit: A Study of the Religious and Charismatic Experience of Jesus and the First Christians as Reflected in the New Testament.* Grand Rapids, Michigan: Eerdmans Publishing.

Engh, M. E. (1992). *Frontier Faiths: Church, Temple and Synagogue in Los Angeles: 1846-1888.* Albuquerque: University of New Mexico Press.

Evanosky, D., & Kos, E. J. (2014). *Lost Los Angeles.* London: Pavilion.

Feinstein, E. (2012). How Can You Sleep? *Sh'ma A Journal of Jewish Ideas.* Retrieved from http://shma.com/2012/09/how-can-you-sleep/

Feldman, F. L. (2003). Human Services in the City of Angels Part I: 1850-1920. *Southern California Quarterly, 85*(2).

Flamming, D. (2005). *Bound for Freedom: Black Los Angeles in the Jim Crow Era.* Berkley, California: University Of California Press.

Frankiel, S. S. (1988). *California's Spiritual Frontiers: Religious Alternatives in Anglo-Protestantism; 1850-1910.* Berkeley, Calif.: Univ. of California Press.

Fuller, D. P. (1972). *Give the Winds a Mighty Voice: The Story of Charles E. Fuller*. New York City: Word.

Graham, B. (1997). *Just As I Am: The Autobiography of Billy Graham*. San Francisco: Zondervan.

Griffis, W. E. (1884). *Korea: The Hermit Nation*. New York: C. Scribners Sons.

Goff, J. (1988). *Fields White unto Harvest: Charles F. Parham and the Missionary Origins of Pentecostalism*. Fayetteville, Arkansas: University of Arkansas Press.

Gutting, G. (2005). *Foucault: A Very Short Introduction*. Oxford: Oxford University Press.

Hallenbeck, C., & Williams, J. H. (1938). *Legends of the Spanish Southwest*. Arthur H. Clark.

Hangen, T. J. (2002). *Redeeming the Dial Radio: Religion, and Popular Culture in America*. Chapel Hill, North Carolina: The University of North Carolina Press.

Harari, Y. N. (2017). *Homo deus: A Brief History of Tomorrow*. New York: Harper.

Heimann, J. (2013). *Los Angeles. Portrait of a city*. Slovakia: Taschen.

Himmelfarb, G. (1987). *The New History and the Old: Critical Essays and Reappraisals*. Cambridge (Mass.): Harvard University Press

History of American Women Blog. *Biddy Mason*. (2017, April 02). Retrieved from http://www.womenhistoryblog.com/2013/05/biddy-mason.html

HLC Filming and Events. (2014, June 16). Immanuel Presbyterian Church (Tour). Retrieved April 11, 2018, from https://www.youtube.com/watch?v=vwLq375IEJI 2

Holiday, R. (2017, May 21). Loving Los Angeles: 36 Books to Help You Finally "Get" LA. Retrieved from https://ryanholiday.net/books-on-los-angeles/

Hunt, D. M., & Ramón, A. (2010). *Black Los Angeles: American Dreams and Racial Realities*. New York: New York University Press.

Immanuel Presbyterian Church Los Angeles (n.d.). Worship & Ministry Services. Retrieved from https://immanuelpres.org/en/

James, G. W. (1904, April). The Founding of the Spanish Missions in California. *The Craftsman*, *VI*(1), 38-48. Retrieved from http://digicoll.library.wisc.edu/cgi-bin/DLDecArts/DLDecArts-idx?type=article&did=DLDecArts.hdv06n01.i0008&id=DLDecArts.hdv06n01&isize=M

Johnson, K. M. (1963). *The Pious Fund*. Los Angeles: Dawsons Book Shop.

Johnston, B. E. (1962). *Californias Gabrielino Indians*. Southwest Museum.

Kegley, H. (1930, June 29). Venice Battle Attests Oil and Water Do Mix. *Los Angeles Times*.

Kelley, R., Friedlander, J., & Colby, A. Y. (Eds.). (1993). *Irangeles: Iranians in Los Angeles*. Berkeley, California: University of California Press.

Kiedis, A., with Flea, Frusciante, J., & Smith, C. (1992). Under the Bridge [Recorded by Red Hot Chili Peppers]. On *Blood Sugar Sex Magik* [Vinyl recording]. Los Angeles: Warner Brothers.

King, Jr., M.L. (1963). "Letter from Birmingham Jail." *Liberation: An Independent Monthly*. Vol. 8 no. 4.

Kurashige, S. (2008). *The Shifting Grounds of Race: Black and Japanese Americans in the Making of Multiethnic Los Angeles*. Princeton, New Jersey: Princeton University Press.

Lah, K. (2017, April 29). The L.A. Riots were a Rude Awakening for Korean Americans. Retrieved from https://www.cnn.com/2017/04/28/us/la-riots-korean-americans/index.html

Latourette, K. S. (1969). *A History of the Expansion of Christianity (Vol. 3)*. New York City: Harper & Row.

Lewis, D. (2013, July 16). Thomas Edison Drove the Film Industry to California. Retrieved from http://mentalfloss.com/article/51722/thomas-edison-drove-film-industry-california

Los Angeles Herald. (1907, October 20). J. L. Griffin Will Open Revival. *Los Angeles Herald*. Vol. 35, No. 18., Retrieved from https://cdnc.ucr.edu/cgi-bin/cdnc?a=d&d=LAH19071020.2.39&e=-------en--20--1--txt-txIN--------1

Löwith, K. (1957). *Meaning in History: The Theological Implications of the Philosophy of History*. Chicago: University of Chicago Press

Luther, C. (2011, January 23). "Jack LaLanne Obituary: Jack LaLanne Dies at 96; Spiritual Father of U.S. Fitness Movement". *Los Angeles Times*.

Martin, D. (2008). *Sacred History and Sacred Geography: Spiritual Journeys in Time and Space*. Vancouver: Regent College.

Mcgee, G. B. (1999). William J. Seymour and the Azusa Street Revival. *The Enrichment Journal,* (Fall). Retrieved from http://enrichmentjournal.ag.org/199904/026_azusa.cfm

McWilliams, C. (1946). *Southern California Country: An Island on the Land*. New York: Duell, Sloan & Pearce.

Meares, H. (2013, March 08). Sign of the Times III: Henry C. Jensen, the Cunning Capitalist of L.A. Retrieved April 5, 2018, from https://www.kcet.org/history-society/sign-of-the-times-iii-henry-c-jensen-the-cunning-capitalist-of-la

Miles, M. R. (1990). *Practicing Christianity: Critical Perspectives for an Embodied Spirituality*. New York, New York: The Crossroads Publishing Company.

Nash, E. (2005, January 29). Don Quixote: The Unlikely Conquistador. Retrieved from https://www.independent.co.uk/arts-entertainment/books/features/don-quixote-the-unlikely-conquistador-488736.html

Newbigin, L. (1981). *Sign of the Kingdom*. Grand Rapids, Michigan: Eerdmans.

Newbigin, L., & Weston, P. (2006). *Lesslie Newbigin: Missionary Theologian: A Reader*. Grand Rapids, Michigan: Eerdmans Publishing

Niebuhr, H. R. (1988). *The Kingdom of God in America*. Middletown, Connecticut: Wesleyan Univ. Press.

O'Conner, L. B. (1997). *Discovering Los Angeles: An Informed Guide to L.A.'s Right and Varied Cultural Life*. Los Angeles: J. Paul Getty Trust.

Okada, V. N. (1998). *Triumphs of Faith: Stories of Japanese-American Christians During World War II*. Los Angeles: Japanese_American Internment Project.

Orr, J. E. (1975). *The Flaming Tongue: Evangelical Awakenings, 1900-*. Chicago: Moody Press.

Owens, R. R. (2005). *The Azusa Street Revival: Its Roots and its Message*. Maitland, Florida: Xulon Press.

Palma, K. (n.d.). Richard Allen: Apostle of Freedom. Retrieved from https://www.sutori.com/story/richard-allen-apostle-of-freedom-9d72ab14-2735-431a-9bdb-b58cb99f4b02

Palóu, F. (1955). Life of Fray Junipero Serra. *Academy of American Franciscan History. Documentary series, v. 3*. Washington: Academy of Amer. Franciscan Hist.

Phillips, J. & Phillips, M. (1963). California Dreamin' [recorded by The Mamas & The Papas] on *If You Can Believe Your Eyes and Ears* [vinyl record]. Hollywood, CA: Dunhill Records.

Pitt, L. (1998). *The Decline of the Californios: A Social History of the Spanish-speaking Californians, 1846-1890*. Berkeley: University of California Press.

Plocheck, R. (2005). Franciscan Missionaries in Texas before 1690. *Texas Almanac*. Texas State Historical Association.

Poloma, M. M. (1972). *Charismatic Movement: Is there a New Pentecost?* Boston: Twayne.

Prescott, W. H. (1847). *Conquest of Peru*. New York: Hurst & Company.

Pronzini, B., & Adrian, J. (Eds.). (1995). *Hard-boiled: An Anthology of American Crime Stories*. Oxford: Oxford University Press. p. 169.

Rashidvash, V. (2013). Iranian People: Iranian Ethnic Groups. *International Journal of Humanities and Social Science, 3*(15), 216-226. Retrieved from http://www.ijhssnet.com/journals/Vol_3_No_15_August_2013/24.pdf

Reid, D. (1994). *Sex, Death, and God in L.A.* Berkeley, CA: University of California Press.

Reid, H., & Heizer, R. F. (1968). *The Indians of Los Angeles County: Hugo Reid's Letters of 1852. Edited and annotated by Robert F. Heizer*. Los Angeles: Southwest Museum Papers No. 21.

Rieff, D. (1992). *Los Angeles: Capital of the Third World*. New York City: Touchstone.

Restall, M., & Fernandez-Armesto, F. (2012). *The Conquistadors*. Oxford: Oxford Univ. Press.

Rimbert, E. (1998, May 30). Junipero Serra Statue Unveiled and Blessed. *Los Angeles Times*. Retrieved from http://articles.latimes.com/1998/may/30/local/me-54783

Robeck, C. M. (2006). *The Azusa Street Mission and Revival: The Birth of the Global Pentecostal Movement*. Nashville, Tennessee: Thomas Nelson.

Robinson, D., & Cooper, A. T. (1998). *Open Hands, Open Heart: The Story of Biddy Mason*. Gardena, CA: Sly Fox Publishing.

Rønde, J. (Director). (2016, June 27). *The DNA Journey feat. Carlos* [Video file]. Retrieved from https://www.youtube.com/watch?v=EYnutforqeY

Saavedra, M. D. (1995). *The History of that Ingenious Gentleman, Don Quijote de la Mancha* (B. Raffel, Trans.). New York: Norton.

Sahagun, L. (2013, October 28). The L.A. Aqueduct at 100. Retrieved from http://graphics.latimes.com/me-aqueduct/

Salomon, C. M. (2010). *Pi´ o Pico: The Last Governor of Mexican California*. Norman, Oklahoma: University of Oklahoma Press.

Sandeen, E. R. (2008). *The Roots of Fundamentalism: British and American Millenarianism, 1800-1930* (Reprint Edition ed.). Chicago: University of Chicago Press.

Sassoon, J. M. (1995). *Jonah* (The Anchor Yale Bible Commentaries). New Haven, Connecticut: Yale University Press.

Schaff, P., & Wace, H. (1893). *A Select Library of the Nicene and Post-Nicene Fathers of the Christian Church: Volume VI, St. Jerome: Letters and Select Works* (Vol. VI, Second). New York City: Christian Literature., Ep. 108.9.

Seymour, W. J., & Martin, L. E. (2000). *The Doctrines and Discipline of the Azusa Street Apostolic Faith Mission of Los Angeles, California*. Joplin, MO: Christian Life Books, the Publishing arm of River of Revival Ministries.

Shackles, C. (Director). (2014, August 14). *The Azusa Street Revival 1906 – Documentary* [Video file]. Available at: https://www.youtube.com/watch?v=VPm980ATPa4

Shenk, W. R., & Plantinga, R. J. (Eds.). (2016). *Christianity & Religious Plurality: Historical and Global Perspectives*. Eugene, Oregon: Cascade Books, an imprint of Wipf and Stock.

Sherwood, Y. (2012). Jonah and Jesus. *Sh'ma: A Journal of Jewish Ideas*, (Sept. 3), p. 8. Retrieved from http://shma.com/2012/09/jonah-and-jesus/

Shin, S., & Ahn-Park, Y. (2017, January 13). Why Are There So Many Korean Missionaries in the U.S., a "Missionaries' Nation"? *The Kukmin Daily*. Retrieved from http://www.kukmindaily.co.kr/article/view.asp?arcid=0011197657

Smale, J., & Welch, T. (2017). *The Pentecostal Blessing: Sermons That Prepared Los Angeles for the Azusa Street Revival* (Spirit Empowered) (C. M. Robeck Jr. & D. Rodgers, Eds.). Springfield, Missouri: Gospel Publishing House.

Smith, D. M. (1974). *John*. Philadelphia: Fortress Press.

Soja, E. W. (2014). *My Los Angeles: From urban restructuring to regional urbanization*. Berkeley, California: Univ. of California Press.

Speer, R. E. (1904). *Missions and Modern History: A Study of the Missionary Aspects of Some Great Movements of the Nineteenth Century*. Grand Rapids, MI: Fleming H. Revell Company

Spencer, T. (1978, November 15). Compton's historic tree has fallen far from glory days. *Los Angeles Times*.

Starr, K., & Ulin, D. L. (2009). *Los Angeles: Portrait of a City* (J. Heimann, Ed.). Los Angeles: Taschen America LLC.

Stevenson, B. E. (2015). *The Contested Murder of Latasha Harlins: Justice, Gender, and the Origins of the LA Riots*. Oxford, England, UK: Oxford University Press.

St. John de Crèvecoeur, J. Hector, J. H. (1963). *Letters from an American Farmer and Sketches of Eighteenth-century America; More Letters from an American Farmer*. New York: American Library.

Surls, R., & Gerber, J. B. (2016). *From Cows to Concrete: The Rise and Fall of Farming in Los Angeles*. Angel City Press.

Summerfield, H., Ryken, L. & Eldredge, L. (2009). "Jonah". Jeffrey, D. L. (Ed.). *A Dictionary of Biblical Tradition in English Literature*. Grand Rapids, MI: W.B. Eerdmans.

Takaki, R. T. (1998). *Strangers from a Different Shore: A History of Asian Americans*. Boston: Little, Brown and Co.

Taylor, J. V. (2004). *The Go-between God (2nd Edition)*. London: SCM Press.

Ulin, D. L. (2002). *Writing Los Angeles: A Literary Anthology*. New York: Literary Classics of the United States.

Vandersloot, J. D. (1988, September 11). The Charges Against Father Junipero Serra. *Los Angeles Times*. Retrieved from http://articles.latimes.com/1988-09-11/local/me-2801_1_father-serra-mission-system-san-juan-capistrano-mission

Volf, M. (2017). *Flourishing: Why We Need Religion in a Globalized World.* New Haven, Connecticut: Yale University Press.

Von Rad, G.(1965). *The Message of the Prophets.* San Francisco: HarperCollins, LLC.

Walls, A. F. (2000, July). Eusebius Tries Again: Reconceiving the Study of Christian history. *International Bulletin of Missionary Research, 24*(3).

Walls, A. F. (2002). *The Missionary Movement in Christian history: Studies in the Transmission of Faith.* Maryknoll, New York: Orbis Books.

Walt Disney. (2016, June 08). Retrieved from https://whenyouwishuponastarblog.wordpress.com/2016/06/08/walt-disney/

Webber, F. J. (1964). Book Review -The Pious Fund by Kenneth Johnson (Los Angeles: Dawson's Book Shop (1963)). Published in *Southern California Quarterly, 46*(1), pp. 93-94. Retrieved from http://scq.ucpress.edu/content/ucpsocal/46/1/93.full.pdf

Weist, The Reverend Derell T. (2009). *Stories of the First Protestant Churches in Los Angeles: 1850-1880.* Self-Published.

Wicher, E. A. (1927). *The Presbyterian Church in California, 1849-1927.* New York: F.H. Hitchcock.

Wolf, A. (1992). "Bibliography of Exclusion and Embrace." From Lamont, M., & Fournier, M. (Eds.). (1992). *Cultivating Differences: Symbolic Boundaries and the Making of Inequality.* Chicago: University of Chicago Press.

Wood, B. A. (1997). *First African Methodist Episcopal Church and its Social Intervention in South Central Los Angeles.* Los Angeles: University of S. Cal.

Yeretzian, A. S., (1974). *A History of Armenian Immigration to America with Special Reference to Los Angeles.* San Francisco: R. & E. Research Associates, 94112 Library of Congress # 73-824000: University of Southern California. (Reprinted from *A History of Armenian Immigration to America with Special Reference to Los Angeles* (Master's thesis, University

Lovejoy

of Southern California). Los Angeles: University of Southern California, (1923)).

Yu, E., Phillips, E. H., & Yang, E. S. (Eds.). (1982). *Koreans in Los Angeles: Prospects and Promises*. Los Angeles: Koryo Research Institute.

Made in the USA
Columbia, SC
06 March 2019